the
pressure
cooker
cookbook

the
pressure
cooker
cookbook

more than 50 recipes for
homemade meals in minutes

Laura Washburn

photography by William Reavell

RYLAND
PETERS
& SMALL
LONDON NEW YORK

Senior designer Sonya Nathoo
Editor Ellen Parnavelas
Production manager Gordana Simakovic
Art director Leslie Harrington
Editorial director Julia Charles

Food stylist and recipe contributor
Maxine Clark
Prop stylist Sue Rowlands
Assistant food stylist Sarah Ackhurst
Indexer Claire Hodgson

Author's Acknowledgements
Special thanks to Rosalind Rathouse of
Cookery School at Little Portland Street
for getting me hooked on pressure cookers,
and also to Richard Ehrlich and his daughter
Rebecca for the loan of additional cookers.

First published in 2012 by
Ryland Peters & Small
20–21 Jockey's Fields
London WC1R 4BW
and
Ryland Peters & Small, Inc.
519 Broadway, 5th Floor
New York NY10012
www.rylandpeters.com

10 9 8 7 6 5 4 3 2 1

Text © Laura Washburn 2012, with
the exception of the recipes on pages
46, 53, 67, 71, 86, 89, 94, 97, 105, 114
© Maxine Clark
All design and photographs
© Ryland Peters & Small 2012

ISBN: 978-1-84975-192-6

A CIP record for this book is available
from the British Library.

US Library of congress cataloging-in-
publication data has been applied for.

Printed and bound in China

Notes
• All spoon measurements are level,
unless otherwise specified.
• Read your pressure cooker manual
before you begin and always use according
to the manufacturer's instructions. Because
pressure cookers vary slightly from
manufacturer to manufacturer, always check
recipe timings with your model's directions
for a recipe using the same ingredients.
• All eggs are medium, unless otherwise
specified. Recipes containing raw or partially
cooked egg, or raw fish or shellfish, should
not be served to the very young, very old,
anyone with a compromised immune
system or pregnant women.

contents

Cooking Under Pressure

Mention the words 'pressure cooker' and most people think of large, antiquated aluminium vessels and ceiling-splattering explosions. However, pressure cookers have come a long way since those days.

The first time I saw a pressure cooker, I was living in France as an exchange student. I stayed with several different families and each one approached cooking differently but they all used pressure cookers. I was curious and keen to learn about cooking, but as much as I liked spending time in the kitchen watching my French host family while they cooked, I was afraid of watching them use the pressure cooker. It was an unfamiliar sight and I found the hissing noises and steam quite frightening. I was always very keen to leave the kitchen when the pressure cooker came out.

It has taken me 30 years to overcome my fear and tackle pressure cooking, but I was determined to try and I am very pleased I did. Pressure cookers are remarkable cooking utensils and my one regret is that it has taken me so long to come round to using them.

Pressure cookers have evolved over time and today they are nothing like the steaming, hissing pots I remember from French kitchens past, though many of my fears were unfounded.

My family never had a pressure cooker when I was a child because I grew up in a warm climate and much of our home cooking was done on the outdoor gas barbecue. With this background, I was not an expert, or even a fan of pressure cooking when I started using one.

As a food writer, I am increasingly aware that while many people enjoy cooking, lack of time is often a problem. I thought it seemed important to find a way to lure time-pressured cooking enthusiasts back into the kitchen and the pressure cooker turned out to be the solution I was looking for.

At the cookery school where I work, we began using pressure cookers because they offer a way to speed up time-consuming tasks such as stewing meat and cooking with dried pulses, because it is often difficult to fit everything into a single class.

As I became accustomed to using pressure cookers for my work, I thought of ways to use them in my home kitchen and the idea of writing a collection of recipes specifically for the pressure cooker was born.

Pressure cookers save time, and we can all do with more of that. A pressure cooker is perhaps the most effective time-saving kitchen utensil you will ever own. It also offers a healthy way to prepare foods by retaining more nutrients thanks to shorter cooking times and it saves energy because the foods cook so quickly. There is no longer any excuse for not using one, and if I can manage it, anyone can.

A POTTED HISTORY

Domestic pressure cookers came into being as a time-saving device based on professional models, but they went out of fashion when demand could not keep up with supply and less reliable cookers came into the market. In North America, the decline came in the 1950s when the market was flooded with poorly produced pressure cookers which resulted in many kitchen disasters. Eventually, many home cooks fell out of love with pressure cookers due to their lack of reliability.

Deemed untrustworthy, pressure cookers were relegated to the backs of kitchen cupboards and other time saving devices and culinary equipment became more fashionable. Speed, however, was still of prime importance and frozen convenience foods and microwaves stepped into the place of the forgotten pressure cooker.

The new generation of pressure cookers are very easy to use and have much more effective safety features. While they have gone out of fashion in North American and some European kitchens, they have long been used in many other places, especially India and North Africa, where their fuel-efficiency and time-saving qualities are highly prized. They are also well suited to the traditional cuisines of these areas as pressure cookers work well for simmering stews and soups containing inexpensive cuts of meat or dried pulses.

In spite of the time-saving advantages, pressure cooking is not a good way to cook everything. A pressure cooker cooks some foods very well, and many things badly so it is important to understand which foods work best to make the most of your pressure cooker.

Pressure cookers are particularly good for tenderizing ingredients, such as dried pulses and cheaper, tough cuts of meat. They are also very good for even steam cooking, as they have the same effect as a bain marie (water bath), only with much shorter cooking times. Delicate ingredients which require a gentle touch or cook quickly, such as asparagus, are best kept far from a pressure cooker as the intense heat and high pressure can often do a lot more harm than good.

HOW PRESSURE COOKERS COOK

Understanding how a pressure cooker works is the key to understanding what types of food will cook well. Pressure cookers are sealed environments. The food cooks as a result of being trapped inside a heated vessel in which steam circulates under pressure. Steam is vital to the process, so any recipe which does not contain liquid already (such as a stew) must have water added (as when steaming vegetables). It is, essentially, a very sophisticated form of steaming. Pressure-cooked foods have all the attributes of steamed food: they are tenderized, moist and more nutritionally sound.

Pressure-cooked foods therefore will not be browned and crispy. If this effect is desired, for example when cooking meat, it must be done before the pressure cooking commences. In most of my recipes, this step has been added, which does slightly increase the time required. For some recipes, it is a necessity that merits a few more minutes at the stove, in my opinion.

The modern palate has become accustomed to intensely flavoured foods. In soups, stews and other dishes made with a pressure cooker, this intensity is generally derived from reducing the cooking liquid, uncovered, over low heat for a long time. This cannot be done under pressure as the liquid stays inside the cooker so no reduction can take place. However, reductions can be done on the stovetop after the cooking is complete, to intensify or thicken any sauces.

When I first started using a pressure cooker, I found many of the recipes bland and watery until I learned how to adjust for this occurrence by seasoning differently. Learning to season pressure-cooked foods is also a skill which takes practice and the best way to master this is to pay attention to the small print. Using lots of fresh herbs to complement your ingredients will help intensify the flavours of pressure cooked recipes. When it says taste and adjust the seasoning at the end of the recipe, it really is necessary if you want to get the most out of your pressure cooker. Adding salt at the end of the cooking time, for example, is vital when using a pressure cooker

Other ways to adjust recipes include adding soy sauce, Worcestershire sauce, or any other intensely flavoured aromatic ingredient which is compatible with the dish, after the pressure has been released. If time is not an issue, liquids or sauces can be reduced after pressure cooking by simply simmering on the stove in the traditional way. Even 5 minutes of additional stovetop cooking will intensify the flavours and sauces can also be thickened by adding a little flour to the reduction.

COOKING VEGETABLES AND PULSES IN A PRESSURE COOKER

Ingredient (all roughly 4 serving sizes)	Approximate Cooking Times
Beetroot/beets, whole	10–20 minutes
Broccoli, stalks and stems	2–4 minutes
Cannellini beans (unsoaked)	30–40 minutes
Carrots	3–5 minutes
Cauliflower, large florets	2–3 minutes
Kidney beans (unsoaked)	30–40 minutes
Leeks, whole	2–4 minutes
Pinto beans (unsoaked)	30–40 minutes
Potatoes, small whole or large quartered	4–7 minutes

EQUIPMENT AND TECHNIQUES

There are a few kitchen items which will help you get the most from your pressure cooker

Kitchen timer

This is absolutely vital when pressure cooking. A good digital timer, with a clear display and loud alarm will ensure timing is accurate.

Heat diffuser

This is a metal trivet-like device which sits over the heat source and under the cooker and helps regulate the temperature. This can be helpful for rice or grain dishes where liquid is absorbed during cooking to prevent scorching.

Springform cake pan

Depending upon the internal diameter of your cooker, you may need a smaller than average pan to prepare some of the recipes in this book. It must be large enough to allow extra room for inserting and removing the pan.

Heatproof bowl

A ceramic soufflé dish is best here, one with straight sides and, again, it needs to fit the internal diameter of your pressure cooker, with just enough extra room to allow for inserting and removing the dish. Using foil to create a handle to allow you to raise and lower the dish (see photographs left) is a useful technique.

Releasing the pressure

This is what I first found most frightening about pressure cookers, but it is very straightforward. There are two ways to do this: cooling down naturally and the quick-cool method. It is important to read manufacturer guidelines for individual models to best understand how to do this for your own pressure cooker.

Natural cool down

To cool down naturally, turn off the heat and leave the lid locked in place until the pressure valve indicates it is safe to release the lid.

Quick cool method

The quick-cool method involves placing part of the pressure cooker under cold running water to speed up the cooling process. Some cookers have a button or lever which will do the same thing as the cold water. Follow the manufacturer's advice on how to achieve this for your particular brand of cooker and never open the cooker until you're sure that it is safe.

Testing the food

To test whether the food is cooked, use the quick-cool method and open when the pressure valve indicates it is safe. If the food requires further cooking, simply lock the lid back in place and return to pressure.

SAFETY GUIDELINES

Please read the instructions for using your particular make and model of pressure cooker carefully before using and follow those specific guidelines for best results.

CHOOSING A PRESSURE COOKER

The recipes in this book are designed to help the ordinary home cook become acquainted with the new generation of pressure cookers. Results may vary according to the manufacturer and the capacity of pressure cooker used for preparation. As with any new technique, it may take a bit of time before the skills are mastered.

Because of the history of pressure cookers and a tendency for cheap mass-produced models to perform poorly, I think it is worth investing in a high-quality and therefore higher priced pressure cooker. The return will be in delicious meals made from generally less expensive ingredients, with lower energy use and increased health benefits.

BIGGER IS BETTER

The size of the pressure cooker you choose is important. Larger pots are more costly, but they also allow for more flexibility. Since the recipes prepared in a pressure cooker are usually intended to serve at least 4 people, it makes

sense to go for a larger size if possible. Smaller portions can always be cooked in a large pot, but not the opposite.

Large pressure cookers tend to be tall and thin and smaller pressure cookers wide and squat. The advantage of a tall thin pot is that it makes it easier to cook small portions, which is not necessarily true of a wide pot. The chances of scorching are also reduced if the surface area of the bottom is reduced. This is not to say that wide pots are not good, they are perfectly effective, only less adaptable. If you only have one pressure cooker, and it is a small capacity, serving sizes will be limited. In the case of pressure cookers, bigger is decidedly better with at least a 6–8 litre/6–8 quart capacity being ideal.

CARING FOR YOUR COOKER

Always follow the manufacturer's guidelines for care and storage of your equipment. However, to prolong the life and increase the function of your pressure cooker, it is always advisable to clean it thoroughly. An old toothbrush can be useful for scrubbing the vent area in particular. Be sure to allow the pressure cooker to dry thoroughly inside and out before storing away as moisture is not good for the durability of the rubber gasket.

soups
& stocks

There is no need to peel the potatoes for this soup which makes preparation even faster – just make sure you scrub them well before dicing. I find this soup perfectly nice as it is but if a smooth texture is preferred, feel free to whizz it with a hand-held blender.

potato and leek soup

1.3 kg/3 lb potatoes
1 large leek
(about 200 g/7 oz)
2 onions, chopped
2 tablespoons butter
1 tablespoon vegetable oil
1 teaspoon dried thyme
leaves from a small bunch
of fresh flat-leaf parsley,
finely chopped
4–5 garlic cloves, sliced
1.5 litres/6 cups chicken
or vegetable stock
(see pages 32–35)
1 bay leaf
Worcestershire sauce,
to taste (optional)
sea salt and freshly ground
black pepper
double/heavy cream or
crème fraîche, to serve

Serves 4

Peel the potatoes if desired then cut them into fine dice.

Split the leek in half lengthwise, wash well and pat dry with paper towels. Slice thinly, using the green part as well as the white.

Combine the leek, onions, butter and oil in the pressure cooker. Set on the stovetop over high heat and cook for 5–8 minutes, stirring occasionally, until coloured.

Add the thyme, parsley, garlic and potatoes and stir to mix. Cook for a further 1–2 minutes before adding the stock, bay leaf and about 1 teaspoonful of salt. (If the stock is already seasoned taste before adding as it may already be salty enough.)

Lock on the lid and bring to high pressure. Lower the heat slightly but maintain high pressure and cook under high pressure for 10 minutes then let cool naturally. When cool, release and remove the lid, taking care of any steam that is expelled as you open the pressure cooker.

Taste and adjust the seasoning, adding Worchestershire sauce if desired and salt and pepper if needed.

To serve, ladle into warmed soup bowls and stir a spoonful of cream into each. Serve immediately.

In my experience, light late-night suppers are difficult to achieve because they also need to be fast to prepare. This is a good recipe to have on hand for just such an occasion as it can be ready in under 30 minutes. That said, it is aromatic and satisfying at any time of day, and about as quick as you get for homemade soup.

Thai chicken soup with noodles

200 g/7 oz wheat or rice
   noodles
250 g/9 oz boneless skinless
   chicken
25-g/1-oz piece of fresh
   ginger, grated
1 lemongrass stalk (white
   part), bruised and finely
   chopped
1 fresh red chilli/chile,
   deseeded and thinly sliced
1 teaspoon red or green
   Thai curry paste
400 ml/1½ cups coconut
   milk
1 litre/4 cups chicken stock
   (see page 35)
3–4 spring onions/scallions,
   thinly sliced on the
   diagonal
1 teaspoon sea salt
1–2 tablespoons Thai fish
   sauce, to taste
freshly squeezed juice
   of 1 lime

To serve
a large handful of fresh
   coriander/cilantro leaves
lime wedges

Serves 2–3

Bring a large saucepan of water to the boil. Add the noodles and cook according to the package instructions. Drain and set aside.

Meanwhile, cut the chicken into small thin strips. Put in the pressure cooker, along with the ginger, lemongrass, chilli/chile, curry paste, coconut milk and stock. Stir to combine.

Lock on the lid and bring to high pressure. Lower the heat slightly but maintain high pressure and cook under high pressure for 5 minutes then let cool naturally. When cool, release and remove the lid, taking care of any steam that is expelled as you open the pressure cooker.

Stir in the sliced spring onions/scallions, cooked noodles, salt and 1 tablespoon of the fish sauce. Let stand for a few minutes. Taste and add more fish sauce as required. Squeeze in the lime juice and stir well.

To serve, ladle into warmed soup bowls and scatter with coriander/cilantro leaves. Serve immediately with lime wedges on the side for squeezing.

This is a very easy recipe, perfect for demonstrating the simplicity of pressure cooking. Unlike many traditional soups, which derive flavour from long, slow open-top simmering, this recipe is so basic that this is achieved by thoroughly browning the onions at the start and using a well-seasoned stock. If using store-bought stock, Worcestershire sauce is a good way to add depth of flavour quickly.

onion soup

4 large onions, halved and thinly sliced
2 tablespoons butter
2 tablespoons vegetable oil
I tablespoon dried thyme
3 garlic cloves, crushed
125 ml/½ cup dry white wine
1.2 litres/5 cups chicken or vegetable stock (see pages 32–35) or beef stock
sea salt and freshly ground black pepper
Worcestershire sauce, to taste (optional)

To serve
finely grated Parmesan
crusty baguette

Serves 4

Combine the onions, butter and oil in the pressure cooker. Set on the stovetop over high heat and cook for at least 10 minutes, stirring occasionally, until well coloured but taking care not to burn. The onions should be deep brown, caramelized and aromatic.

Stir in the thyme, garlic and wine and bring to the boil. Boil for 1 minute to cook off the alcohol. If your stock is unseasoned, or lightly seasoned, add about 1 teaspoon salt, or more to taste.

Add the stock. Lock on the lid and bring to high pressure. Lower the heat slightly but maintain high pressure and cook under high pressure for 7 minutes then let cool naturally. When cool, release and remove the lid, taking care of any steam that is expelled as you open the pressure cooker.

Taste and adjust the seasoning, adding Worcestershire sauce if desired. To serve, ladle into warmed soup bowls and sprinkle with finely grated Parmesan. Serve immediately with thick slices of crusty baguette.

Variation: A spoonful or so of good quality ready-made pesto sauce added just before serving makes a nice change and really lifts the flavour.

Growing up, my favourite convenience food was a popular brand of canned Italian-style soups and lentil was decidedly the best. I never touch canned soup now, but this recipe pays hommage to fond memories of childhood meals. As with all soups prepared in a pressure cooker, the taste will be determined by the stock so be sure it is well seasoned.

lentil soup with spinach

1 onion, finely chopped
1 carrot, diced
2 tablespoons olive or vegetable oil
1 teaspoon dried thyme
3 garlic cloves, sliced
125 ml/½ cup dry white wine
1.5 litres/6 cups chicken or vegetable stock (see pages 32–35)
300 g/1½ cups dried Puy/French lentils
225 g/1 cup canned chopped tomatoes
150 g/5 cups fresh spinach leaves, washed and finely chopped
a large handful of chopped fresh basil or flat-leaf parsley
sea salt and freshly ground black pepper
crusty baguette, to serve

Serves 2–4

Combine the onions, carrot and oil in the pressure cooker. Set on the stovetop over high heat and cook for at least 10 minutes, stirring occasionally, until well coloured but taking care not to burn. The vegetables should be deep brown, caramelized and aromatic.

Stir in the thyme, garlic and wine and bring to the boil. Boil for 1 minute to cook off the alcohol.

Add the stock and lentils. Lock on the lid and bring to high pressure. Lower the heat slightly but maintain high pressure and cook under high pressure for 10 minutes. Cool down using the quick cool method. When cool, release and remove the lid, taking care of any steam that is expelled as you open the pressure cooker.

Stir in the tomatoes and spinach and cook over high heat, without the lid, for 2–3 minutes, just to warm through and wilt the spinach. Stir in the basil or parsley.

Taste and adjust the seasoning. To serve, ladle into warmed soup bowls and serve immediately with chunks of crusty baguette.

Dried beans are economical and nutritious but I have always found the planning of pre-soaking impossible to manage. Pressure cookers have revolutionized the way I use dried beans and now that I don't have to soak them, I use them all the time. This is a showcase recipe for my new-found skill. It is simple, straightforward and sublime, thanks to a few basic ingredients, lots of fresh herbs and, of course, the pressure cooker!

bean and bacon soup with garlic and fresh herbs

I large onion, finely chopped

I large carrot, finely chopped

2 celery stalks, finely chopped

I tablespoon olive oil

200 g/7 oz bacon, coarsely chopped

4–6 garlic cloves, sliced

a small bunch of fresh flat-leaf parsley, finely chopped

leaves from a few sprigs of fresh thyme, finely chopped

leaves from 2 sprigs of fresh oregano, finely chopped

leaves from I small sprig of fresh rosemary, finely chopped

1.2 litres/5 cups chicken or vegetable stock (see pages 32–35)

200 g/1 cup dried haricot or cannellini beans

I bay leaf

sea salt and freshly ground black pepper

a drizzle of extra virgin olive oil, to serve

Serves 4

Combine the onion, carrot, celery and oil in the pressure cooker. Set on the stovetop over high heat and cook for at least 10 minutes, stirring occasionally, until well coloured but taking care not to burn. The vegetables should be deep brown, caramelized and aromatic.

Stir in the bacon, garlic, parsley, thyme, oregano and rosemary and cook for 1–2 minutes more, until browned.

Add the stock, beans and bay leaf. Lock on the lid and bring to high pressure. Lower the heat slightly but maintain high pressure and cook the soup under high pressure for 40 minutes. Cool down using the quick cool method. When cool, release and remove the lid, taking care of any steam that is expelled as you open the pressure cooker.

Taste the beans. If they are not completely tender, repeat the pressure cooking process for a further 10 minutes.

Remove 4 large spoonfuls of beans and vegetables and set aside. Using a hand-held blender or food processor, blend the soup until smooth. Taste and adjust the seasoning. To serve, ladle into warmed soup bowls, adding a spoonful of the reserved beans and vegetables to each bowl. Drizzle with olive oil, if using, and serve immediately.

This is a fantastic all-purpose vegetable soup made more substantial with the addition of beans and pasta. The recipe is not the quickest in the book, but it is very easy nonetheless.

minestrone

2 tablespoons olive or vegetable oil
1 large onion, finely diced
2 celery stalks, finely diced
1 large carrot, finely diced
1 teaspoon dried thyme
3–5 garlic cloves, thinly sliced
250 ml/1 cup red or white wine
1.5 litres/6 cups chicken or vegetable stock (see pages 32–35)
140 g/⅔ cup dried haricot or cannellini beans
225 g/8 oz canned chopped tomatoes
1 small courgette/ zucchini, diced
100 g/⅔ cup green beans, diced
50 g/½ cup small dried pasta or broken spaghetti
1 teaspoon sea salt
1 teaspoon sugar (optional)
a large handful each of chopped fresh flat-leaf parsley and basil

To serve
finely grated Parmesan
freshly ground black pepper

Serves 6–8

Combine the oil, onion, celery and carrot in the pressure cooker. Set on the stovetop over medium-high heat and cook for at least 10 minutes, stirring occasionally, until well coloured but taking care not to burn. The vegetables should be deep brown, caramelized and aromatic.

Stir in the thyme, garlic and wine and bring to the boil. Boil for 1 minute to cook off the alcohol.

Stir in the stock and haricot beans. Lock on the lid and bring to high pressure. Lower the heat slightly but maintain high pressure and cook under high pressure for 30 minutes then let cool naturally. When cool, release and remove the lid, taking care of any steam that is expelled as you open the pressure cooker.

Add the salt, tomatoes, courgette/zucchini, green beans and pasta. Lock on the lid and bring to high pressure. Lower the heat slightly but maintain high pressure and cook under high pressure for 1 minute. Cool down using the quick cool method.

Taste and adjust the seasoning. Add sugar to taste if the tomatoes make the soup too acidic. To serve, stir in the fresh herbs and ladle into warmed soup bowls. Top with grated Parmesan and freshly ground black pepper and serve immediately.

If you have any wilted or less than fresh vegetables around, the stock pot is the perfect place for them. All those listed here are requisite for a well-flavoured stock, especially the mushrooms. It is also important to brown the onions and other aromatics at the outset as this adds to the taste of the stock. Other vegetables to try include broccoli, potatoes, spring onions/scallions and courgettes/zucchini, as well as any fresh or dried herbs.

vegetable stock

2 large onions, coarsely
    chopped, skins reserved
1 leek, coarsely chopped
4 carrots, coarsely chopped
3 celery stalks, with leaves,
    coarsely chopped
2–3 tablespoons olive or
    vegetable oil
200 g/2 cups coarsely
    chopped mushrooms
1 parsnip or swede/
    rutabaga, coarsely
    chopped (optional)
4 garlic cloves, unpeeled
    and halved
a small bunch of fresh
    flat-leaf parsley, torn
a few sprigs of fresh thyme
1 bay leaf
2 teaspoons sea salt
a few whole black
    peppercorns
Worcestershire sauce,
    or soy sauce, to taste
    (optional)

Makes about 1.5 litres/
    6 cups

Put the onions, leek, carrots, celery and oil in the pressure cooker and set on the stovetop over medium-high heat until the oil begins to sizzle. Cook the vegetables until browned. Do not stir them too often or they will not brown adequately.

Add the mushrooms and parsnip, if using, and cook for 3–5 minutes, until browned.

Stir in the garlic and cook for 1 minute. Add at least 1.5 litres/ 6 cups water or enough to cover the vegetables by about 2 cm/¾ in. Stir in the reserved onion skins for extra colour, and add the herbs, salt and peppercorns.

Lock on the lid and bring to high pressure. Lower the heat slightly but maintain high pressure and cook under high pressure for 10 minutes then let cool naturally. When cool, release and remove the lid, taking care of any steam that is expelled as you open the pressure cooker.

Strain the stock. Taste and adjust the seasoning, adding salt if needed. For more depth of flavour, add Worcestershire or soy sauce, 1 tablespoon at a time, as desired.

The stock can be frozen or kept covered in the refrigerator for up to 1 week. Bring to a rolling boil before using.

Pressure cookers offer a way to make a very flavoursome stock in no time at all and chicken stock is perhaps my favourite. If you can get a tough old bird for the stock pot, even better, as the meat will be perfectly tenderized under pressure and can be shredded for use in pies, soups or salads.

chicken stock

1.5–1.8 kg/3.5–4 lb chicken, whole or cut into 6 pieces
2 large onions, unpeeled and coarsely chopped
2 carrots, coarsely chopped
3 celery stalks with leaves, coarsely chopped
4 garlic cloves, unpeeled and halved
a small bunch of fresh flat-leaf parsley, torn
a few sprigs of fresh thyme
1 bay leaf
2 teaspoons sea salt
a few whole black peppercorns

Makes 1–2 litres/4–8 cups

Combine all of the ingredients in the pressure cooker and add enough water to cover by about 2 cm/¾ in.

Lock on the lid and bring to high pressure. Lower the heat slightly but maintain high pressure and cook under high pressure for 30 minutes then let cool naturally. When cool, release and remove the lid, taking care of any steam that is expelled as you open the pressure cooker.

Strain the stock. Taste and adjust the seasoning, adding salt if needed. To degrease the stock, refrigerate overnight, then remove the fat from the surface before reheating and using.

The stock can be frozen or kept covered in the refrigerator for up to a week. Bring to a rolling boil before using.

meat

Cooking kidney beans from dried requires a little more time but the resulting deep crimson stew is well worth the wait. The taste is also more earthy than chili con carne made with cooked beans from a can. However, if you want to speed things up, feel free to use canned beans (see variation below).

beef chili con carne

2 tablespoons vegetable oil
650 g/1½ lbs stewing beef,
  cut into small cubes
I large onion, diced
2 red, orange or yellow bell
  peppers, diced
2 celery stalks, diced
I fresh green chilli/chile,
  deseeded and finely
  chopped
3 garlic cloves, crushed
2 teaspoons dried oregano
2 teaspoons ground cumin
125 ml/½ cup red wine
350 g/2 cups dried kidney
  beans
500 ml/2 cups beef stock
400-g/14-oz can chopped
  tomatoes
I bay leaf
1–2 tablespoons sugar,
  to taste (optional)
sea salt and freshly ground
  black pepper

To serve
Tabasco sauce
sour cream
grated cheese
spring onions/scallions,
  sliced on the diagonal

Serves 4–6

Heat 1 tablespoon of the oil in the pressure cooker until hot but not smoking. Add the beef and cook on the stovetop for about 5 minutes, until browned. You may need to brown the beef in batches depending on the size of your pressure cooker as the meat should fit in a fairly even layer. Transfer the browned meat to a plate and set aside.

Add the remaining oil, onion, peppers and celery to the pressure cooker and brown for 5–8 minutes. Stir in the chilli/chile, garlic, oregano and cumin and cook for another minute. Add the wine and boil for 1 minute to allow the alcohol to evaporate.

Add the browned beef, beans, stock, tomatoes and bay leaf to the pressure cooker and stir to mix. Lock on the lid and bring to high pressure. Lower the heat slightly but maintain high pressure. Cook under high pressure for 50 minutes then let cool naturally. When the chili is ready, release and remove the lid, taking care of any steam that is expelled as you open the pressure cooker.

Taste and adjust the seasoning, adding salt to taste and sugar to relieve any bitterness, if needed. Serve topped with sour cream, grated cheese and sliced spring onions/scallions.

Variation: Replace the dried beans with two 400-g/14-oz cans of drained, cooked kidney beans. The method is the same but cook under high pressure for just 20 minutes and let cool down naturally.

This rich-tasting pasta sauce takes much less time to prepare than a conventional one. The traditional Bolognese recipe uses a combination of pork and beef but in this quick-cook version, bacon helps to achieve the same delicious taste and unctuous texture.

bolognese sauce

2 tablespoons olive or
  vegetable oil
I large onion, finely
  chopped
3 celery stalks, finely
  chopped
2 large carrots, peeled and
  finely chopped
3 slices smoked bacon,
  finely chopped
I teaspoon dried thyme
4 garlic cloves, finely
  chopped
500 g/I lb 2 oz beef
  mince/ground beef
2 teaspoons sea salt
125 ml/½ cup red or white
  wine
2 litres/8 cups passata
  (Italian sieved tomatoes)
I bay leaf
I tablespoon sugar
sea salt and freshly ground
  black pepper

To serve
cooked spaghetti
a handful of small fresh
  basil leaves
finely grated Parmesan
  (optional)

Serves 6–8

Combine the oil, onion, celery, carrots and bacon in the pressure cooker. Set on the stovetop over medium-high heat and cook for at least 10 minutes, stirring occasionally, until well coloured but taking care not to burn. The vegetables should be deep brown, caramelized and aromatic.

Stir in the thyme, garlic and beef and cook for 3–5 minutes, stirring occasionally, until browned. Add the salt and wine and bring to the boil. Boil for 1 minute to cook off the alcohol.

Add the passata, bay leaf and sugar and stir well. Lock on the lid and bring to high pressure. Lower the heat slightly but maintain high pressure and cook under high pressure for 30 minutes then let cool naturally. When cool, release and remove the lid, taking care of any steam that is expelled as you open the pressure cooker.

Taste and adjust the seasoning. Spoon into warmed serving bowls of hot spaghetti and serve sprinkled with fresh basil leaves.

Note: This sauce freezes very well in large or small batches so if you have a large capacity pressure cooker, you can double the recipe and keep some for another time.

Pressure cookers are invaluable when preparing tough cuts of meat. Lamb shanks normally require hours of simmering to get them tender enough to fall off the fork but here it only takes an hour to achieve the same result. In no time at all, you will have a meltingly succulent stew on the table, even on a working weeknight.

lamb shank stew with potatoes

2 tablespoons olive or vegetable oil

1.5 kg/3 lbs 5 oz lamb shanks (about 4)

1 large onion, coarsely chopped

350 g/2 cups peeled and thickly sliced carrots

1 generous teaspoon dried thyme

4 garlic cloves, sliced

1 teaspoon sea salt

125 ml/½ cup red or white wine

1 litre/4 cups passata (Italian sieved tomatoes)

1 bay leaf

1.5 kg/3 lbs potatoes

a large handful of fresh flat-leaf parsley or basil leaves, chopped

sea salt and freshly ground black pepper

Serves 4

Heat the oil in the pressure cooker and add the lamb shanks. Cook for about 5 minutes on the stovetop until evenly browned, tuning halfway through cooking time. You may find it easier to work in batches. Remove the browned meat from the pressure cooker, season well with salt and set aside.

Put the onion and carrots in the pressure cooker. Set over medium-high heat and cook for at least 10 minutes, stirring occasionally, until well coloured but taking care not to burn. The vegetables should be deep brown, caramelized and aromatic.

Stir in the thyme, garlic, salt and wine and bring to the boil. Boil for 1 minute to cook off the alcohol.

Stir in the passata and the bay leaf and arrange the lamb on top, making sure each shank is nestled in the sauce. Lock on the lid and bring to high pressure. Lower the heat slightly but maintain high pressure and cook under high pressure for 30 minutes. Cool down using the quick cool method.

While the lamb is cooking prepare the potatoes. Peel if desired and quarter or halve, depending on size. Set aside until needed.

When the lamb is ready, release and remove the lid, taking care of any steam that is expelled as you open the pressure cooker.

Arrange the potatoes on top of the lamb in the pressure cooker, lock the lid back on and return to high pressure. Lower the heat slightly but maintain high pressure and cook under high pressure for 20 minutes. Cool down using the quick cool method. When ready, release and remove the lid, taking care of any steam that is expelled as you open the pressure cooker.

Taste and adjust the seasoning. Put a lamb shank on each serving plate and surround with the vegetables, potatoes and sauce. Garnish with chopped parsley or basil and serve immediately.

This classic recipe is always a crowd-pleaser. Forming the mixture into larger meatballs is much faster than preparing lots of small ones and they still cook just as quickly.

meatballs in tomato, fennel and red pepper sauce

1 onion, sliced
1 fennel bulb, sliced
1 red bell pepper, deseeded and sliced
2 tablespoons vegetable oil
1 teaspoon sea salt
½ teaspoon dried thyme
125 ml/½ cup red wine
500 ml/2 cups passata (Italian sieved tomatoes)
a pinch of sugar
a handful of fresh flat-leaf parsley or basil, chopped
sea salt and freshly ground black pepper

For the meatballs
1 onion, grated
4 cloves garlic, crushed
½ teaspoon fennel seeds, crushed
800 g/1 lb 12 oz mixture of minced/ground beef and pork or all beef
70 g/1 cup fresh breadcrumbs
2 teaspoons sea salt
1 teaspoon sweet paprika
a pinch of dried chilli/hot pepper flakes
1 egg, beaten

To serve
crusty bread
chopped fresh flat-leaf parsley or basil

Serves 4–5

To make the sauce, put the onion, fennel, pepper and oil in the pressure cooker. Set on the stovetop over medium-high heat and cook for at least 10 minutes, stirring occasionally, until well coloured but taking care not to burn. The vegetables should be caramelized and aromatic.

Stir in the salt and thyme and cook for another minute. Add the wine and boil for 1 minute to cook off the alcohol. Stir in the passata and sugar and mix well. Taste and adjust the seasoning and stir in the parsley or basil. Let stand and prepare the meatballs.

Put all the meatball ingredients in a large bowl and mix well to combine. Using your hands, form the mixture into 9–10 balls. Arrange the meatballs in the pressure cooker, on top of the sauce, starting with a bottom row and building up in concentric circles.

Lock on the lid and bring to high pressure. Lower the heat slightly but maintain high pressure and cook under high pressure for 10 minutes then let cool naturally. When cool, release and remove the lid, taking care of any steam that is expelled as you open the pressure cooker.

Spoon onto warmed serving plates and scatter with chopped parsley or basil. Serve with chunks of crusty bread.

This is a fantastic and fast way to cook a cheaper cut of lamb. The meat will be thoroughly cooked through and meltingly tender, as if it has been slow-roasted for hours. The garlic inside will be as soft as butter and the anchovy just melts into the meat, disappearing completely but acting as a seasoning with the capers.

'slow-cooked' lamb with rosemary, garlic, anchovies and capers

1.5 kg/3 lbs 5 oz boned shoulder of lamb
leaves stripped from 2–3 large sprigs of rosemary
4 large garlic cloves, halved lengthways
8 canned anchovy fillets, rinsed
8–12 small salted capers, rinsed
2 tablespoons olive oil
3 carrots, roughly chopped
1 red onion, quartered
3 celery stalks, roughly chopped
200 ml/¾ cup red wine
freshly ground black pepper

To serve
baked or roast potatoes
Ratatouille (see page 86)

Serves 4–6

Unroll the meat skin-side down on a clean work surface. Cut out any large pieces of excess fat. Scatter over a handful of rosemary then spread the garlic pieces over the top. Place the anchovies over the rosemary and garlic, and scatter over the capers. Season with plenty of black pepper but no salt as the anchovies and capers should make it salty enough.

Next, either roll the meat up like a Swiss/jelly roll from the shorter side, or pull all the edges up and towards the middle to form a dome. Using kitchen twine, tie the meat tightly, starting in the middle and working towards each end to give a tidy joint.

Heat the oil in the pressure cooker and add the meat. Cook for 5 minutes on the stovetop until evenly browned, turning halfway through. Remove the meat, season well and set aside.

Place the trivet in the base of the pressure cooker and put the joint on top. Push the carrots, onion and celery around the meat with the remaining rosemary and pour over the wine. Lock on the lid and bring to high pressure. Lower the heat slightly but maintain high pressure and cook under high pressure for 50 minutes. Cool down using the quick cool method. When cool, release and remove the lid, taking care of any steam that is expelled as you open the pressure cooker.

Lift the lamb onto a warm carving dish or board, cover loosely with foil and a thick kitchen towel and leave to rest in a warm place for 30–45 minutes before carving.

Strain the juices into a jug/pitcher and skim off any fat from the surface. If you like a more concentrated gravy, pour the juices into a pan and boil hard to reduce until it tastes right. Keep warm. Once the lamb has rested, remove the twine and carve into generous slices. Serve with potatoes and Ratatouille.

This classic stew is made succulent and tender by the pressure cooker in about an hour. Here it is served with potatoes and carrots, also cooked under pressure, but mashed potatoes or pappardelle would also make good sides and soak up the delicious gravy.

pot roast of brisket with wine, bacon and herbs

1 tablespoon vegetable oil
500 g/1 lb 2 oz beef brisket
1 onion, chopped
1 large carrot, chopped
1 celery stalk, chopped
2–3 slices smoked bacon, chopped
3–4 garlic cloves, chopped
1 teaspoon sea salt
250 ml/1 cup red wine
400-g/14-oz can chopped tomatoes
a 'bouquet garni' of fresh herbs such as thyme, rosemary, parsley and oregano
water or stock, as required
1 bay leaf
chopped fresh flat-leaf parsley, to serve
sea salt and freshly ground black pepper

For the side vegetables (optional)
600 g/1 lb 5 oz small new potatoes, scrubbed
400 g/14 oz thin whole carrots, peeled

Serves 4–6

Heat the oil in the pressure cooker and add the beef. Cook on the stovetop for about 5 minutes until evenly browned, turning halfway through cooking time. Remove the browned meat, season well with salt and set aside.

Put the onion, carrot and celery in the pressure cooker. Set over medium-high heat and cook for at least 10 minutes, stirring occasionally, until well coloured but taking care not to burn. The vegetables should be deep brown, caramelized and aromatic.

Stir in the bacon, garlic and salt and cook for 1–2 minutes. Add the wine, tomatoes, bouquet garni and bay leaf and bring to the boil. Boil for 1 minute to cook off the alcohol.

Place the meat on top of the tomato mixture, nestling the pieces of beef in the sauce. Add enough water or stock to almost cover the meat. Lock on the lid and bring to high pressure. Lower the heat slightly but maintain high pressure and cook under high pressure for 60 minutes. Cool down using the quick cool method. When cool, release and remove the lid, taking care of any steam that is expelled as you open the pressure cooker.

After 60 minutes cooking time, arrange the potatoes and carrots (if using) on top of the beef, lock the lid back on and return to high pressure. Lower the heat slightly but maintain high pressure and cook under high pressure for 6 minutes. Cool down using the quick cool method. When cool, release and remove the lid, taking care of any steam that is expelled as you open the pressure cooker.

Taste and adjust the seasoning. Remove the brisket and slice. Divide the meat slices, side vegetables and sauce between warmed serving plates, sprinkle with chopped parsley and serve immediately.

A few of the chefs at the cooking school where I work have also become pressure cooker converts. This recipe is inspired by one of my colleagues who is very talented when it comes to pasta dishes.

sausage sauce for gnocchi

1 onion, finely chopped
1 large carrot, finely chopped
1–2 tablespoons olive oil
leaves stripped from 1 sprig of fresh rosemary, finely chopped
leaves stripped from 1–2 sprigs of fresh thyme, or ½ teaspoon dried thyme
½ teaspoon dried chilli/hot pepper flakes (optional)
6 Italian- or Toulouse-style sausages (400 g/14 oz), casings removed and broken into pieces
3–4 garlic cloves, crushed
125 ml/½ cup red wine
1 litre/4 cups passata (Italian sieved tomatoes)
½ teaspoon sugar
leaves from a few sprigs of fresh flat-leaf parsley, finely chopped
sea salt and freshly ground black pepper

To serve
500 g/1 lb 2 oz fresh gnocchi
Parmesan shavings

Serves 4

Combine the onion, carrot and oil in the pressure cooker. Set over medium-high heat and cook on the stovetop for at least 10 minutes, stirring occasionally, until well coloured but taking care not to burn. The vegetables should be deep brown, caramelized and aromatic.

Stir in the rosemary, thyme and chilli/hot pepper flakes (if using) and cook for 1–2 minutes until aromatic. Add the sausage pieces and cook for about 5 minutes until browned, stirring occasionally to break up the pieces. Add the garlic and cook for 1 minute. Pour in the wine and bring to the boil. Boil for 1 minute to cook off the alcohol.

Add the passata, 125 ml/½ cup water and the sugar and stir well. Lock on the lid and bring to high pressure. Lower the heat slightly but maintain high pressure and cook under high pressure for 20 minutes then let cool naturally. When cool, release and remove the lid, taking care of any steam that is expelled as you open the pressure cooker.

While the sauce is cooking, prepare the gnocchi according to the package instructions.

Stir the chopped parsley into the sauce. Taste and adjust the seasoning. Divide the cooked gnocchi between warmed serving plates and spoon over the sauce. Top with shavings of Parmesan and serve immediately.

This easily-prepared dish is perfect for a winter's night, especially when served with its traditional accompaniments of gremolata and risotto. Thick-cut veal usually takes over an hour to cook, but in the pressure cooker, it only takes 20 minutes. What is more, it can be made the day before and reheated in the oven.

osso bucco

4 thick-cut slices of veal shin cut for 'osso bucco'
about 4 tablespoons seasoned plain/ all-purpose flour
3 tablespoons olive oil or butter
150 ml/⅔ cup dry white wine
400-g/14-oz can chopped tomatoes
2 teaspoons dried oregano
400 ml/1½ cups chicken or veal stock
sea salt and freshly ground black pepper

For the gremolata
1 garlic clove, finely chopped
4 tablespoons chopped fresh flat-leaf parsley
finely grated zest of 1 small unwaxed lemon

Serves 4

Dip the veal in the seasoned flour and shake off the excess. Heat the oil or butter in the base of the pressure cooker and brown the meat on the stovetop on all sides, two slices at a time.

Remove the meat and set aside. Pour in the wine and stir in the tomatoes and oregano. Bring to the boil and boil hard for 5 minutes to cook off the alcohol.

Return the veal to the pressure cooker and pour in the stock. Season well with salt and pepper.

Lock on the lid and bring to high pressure. Lower the heat slightly but maintain high pressure and cook under high pressure for 20 minutes. Cool down using the quick cool method. When cool, release and remove the lid, taking care of any steam that is expelled as you open the pressure cooker. The meat should be very tender. Baste the veal with the sauce.

If the sauce is too runny, remove the meat and keep warm. Boil the sauce hard to reduce to the desired thickness.

Meanwhile, make the gremolata. Crush the garlic and mix well with the chopped parsley and lemon zest.

Serve with a generous helping of sauce spooned over the meat and a simple risotto (if desired). Sprinkle each plate with the gremolata 5 minutes before serving to release the aromas.

My son loves ribs so I make these often, though rarely on the barbecue since we do not have that sort of climate. Using the pressure cooker, you can make succulent, tender ribs which only need a brief blast of direct heat from the grill/broiler to crisp the tops before serving – much quicker than cooking them in the oven and just as delicious!

pork loin ribs with barbecue sauce

2 kg/4 lbs 8 oz pork loin ribs, cut into 3–4 rib sections
125–250 ml/½–1 cup ready-made barbecue sauce, for basting
spring onions/scallions finely sliced on the diagonal, to serve
sea salt

For the marinade
250 ml/1 cup ready-made barbecue sauce
1 tablespoon clear honey
freshly squeezed juice of 1 orange
2 tablespoons soy sauce

Serves 2–4

To make the marinade, combine the barbecue sauce, honey, orange juice and soy sauce in a large bowl and mix well.

Sprinkle the ribs lightly with salt, then put in the bowl with the marinade and mix to coat well. Put 250 ml/1 cup water in the bottom of the pressure cooker and arrange the rib pieces on top.

Lock on the lid and bring to high pressure. Lower the heat slightly but maintain high pressure and cook under high pressure for 20 minutes then let cool naturally. When cool, release and remove the lid, taking care of any steam that is expelled as you open the pressure cooker. Meanwhile, preheat the grill/broiler.

Remove the ribs from the pressure cooker and transfer to a heavy baking sheet. Brush with the barbecue sauce and grill/broil under a hot grill/broiler for 5–10 minutes to brown the tops. Serve hot, scattered with sliced spring onions/scallions.

Note: To give the ribs a more intense flavour, leave them to marinate in the marinade (covered in the refrigerator) overnight or even for a few hours.

Pork is notorious for taking a long time to cook – not in the pressure cooker! The herbs and milk combine together to make a rich and creamy sauce.

pork cooked in milk with rosemary and bay

1.5 kg/3 lbs 5 oz boneless loin of pork, neatly tied with kitchen twine

2 tablespoons olive oil

4 tablespoons butter

5 garlic cloves, peeled and halved

2 sprigs fresh rosemary

2 fresh bay leaves

3 tablespoons dry white wine

600 ml/2⅓ cups whole milk

1 wide strip pared, unwaxed orange zest

sea salt and freshly ground black pepper

a few sprigs of fresh rosemary, to serve

Serves 4–6

Season the pork all over with salt and pepper. Pour the oil into the base of the pressure cooker and set over medium-high heat. Add the pork and cook for 10 minutes to seal all over, until well browned on all sides. Lift the pork onto a large plate and set aside. Pour away any excess fat and wipe out the pressure cooker with paper towels.

Next, melt the butter in the pressure cooker over medium heat. Add the garlic, rosemary, bay leaves and wine and cook, stirring frequently, until the garlic begins to brown.

Add the pork and any juices from the plate, then add the milk, and tuck in the orange zest.

Lock on the lid and bring to high pressure. Lower the heat slightly but maintain high pressure and cook under high pressure for 40 minutes. Cool down naturally. When cool, release and remove the lid, taking care of any steam that is expelled as you open the pressure cooker.

Lift the meat onto a warm carving dish or board. Don't worry if the juices in the pressure cooker look curdled – this is normal. Taste and adjust the seasoning and remove the herbs. Blend the sauce with a hand-held blender for a smoother texture and thicken with a little cornflour/cornstarch, if liked. To serve, cut the pork into thick slices and cover with the rich sauce. Garnish with sprigs of rosemary and serve immediately.

poultry
& seafood

Like all the recipes in this book, this a simple indication of how to prepare a familiar dish using a pressure cooker. Chicken can be prepared quickly on a stovetop using conventional cooking, but this pressure cooker method tenderizes the meat so it takes on the texture and feel of chicken that has been simmered for hours, not just 15 minutes.

chicken stewed in wine with onions and bacon

2 tablespoons vegetable or olive oil
2 onions, halved and sliced
1.3 kg/3 lbs chicken pieces with bones
a few sprigs of fresh thyme
3–4 garlic cloves, sliced
85 g/⅓ cup bacon lardons
2 teaspoons sea salt
125 ml/½ cup dry white wine
1 bay leaf
sea salt and freshly ground black pepper

To serve
steamed courgette/zucchini
creamy mashed potatoes
chopped fresh flat-leaf parsley

Serves 4

Put the oil and onions in the pressure cooker. Set on the stovetop over medium-high heat and cook for at least 10 minutes, stirring occasionally, until well coloured but taking care not to burn. The onions should be deep brown, caramelized and aromatic. Transfer to a plate, season with salt and set aside.

Add the chicken pieces to the cooker in a single layer and cook for 5–8 minutes, turning once, until browned on both sides. Depending on the size of your cooker, you may need to work in batches. Transfer to a plate, season with salt and set aside.

Return the onions to the cooker. Add the thyme, garlic and bacon and stir to scrape up any browned bits. Cook for 2–3 minutes, until the bacon just browns. Add the salt and wine and bring to the boil. Boil for 1 minute to cook off the alcohol.

Return the browned chicken to the cooker and add the bay leaf. Lock on the lid and bring to high pressure. Lower the heat slightly but maintain high pressure and cook under high pressure for 15 minutes then let cool naturally. When ready, release the lid, taking care of steam that is expelled when removing.

Taste and adjust the seasoning. Divide the chicken pieces between warmed serving plates, pour over a generous amount of sauce and sprinkle with chopped parsley. Serve with courgettes/zucchini and mashed potatoes.

Variations: You can add a small can of chopped tomatoes, some quartered mushrooms or leeks instead of (or as well as) the onions. For Tarragon Chicken, omit the bacon, garlic and bay leaf and stir in a large handful of chopped fresh tarragon and a few spoonfuls of cream before serving.

Pressure cookers really come into their own when making the popular Moroccan stew known as a tagine. All the ingredients are simply combined and cooked together. This recipe is a tremendous treat when served on the day it is made, but it can also be prepared ahead of time which really brings out the rich flavours.

chicken and chickpea tagine

1.8 kg/4 lbs chicken pieces (thighs and breasts, with bones)
200 g/1 cup dried chickpeas
1 large onion, grated or finely chopped in a food processor
2 teaspoons sea salt
1½ teaspoons ground ginger
1½ teaspoons freshly ground black pepper
a pinch of saffron
1 teaspoon turmeric
a small bunch of fresh coriander/cilantro, chopped
¼ teaspoon ground cinnamon
70 g/½ cup sultanas/golden raisins
1 generous tablespoon clear honey

To serve
cooked couscous
lemon wedges
chopped fresh coriander/ cilantro leaves

Serves 4–6

Combine all the ingredients, except the honey, in the pressure cooker and add 1 litre/4 cups water. Stir to mix.

Lock on the lid and bring to high pressure. Lower the heat slightly but maintain high pressure and cook under high pressure for 40 minutes then let cool naturally. When ready, release and remove the lid, taking care of any steam that is expelled as you open the pressure cooker.

Test the chickpeas. If they are not quite done, repeat the pressure cooking process for a further 10 minutes.

Remove the chicken pieces and bring the sauce to the boil. Boil the liquid for 10 minutes to reduce it slightly. Stir in the honey, taste and adjust the seasoning as required. Divide the couscous between warmed serving plates, top with the chicken and sauce and sprinkle with chopped coriander/cilantro. Serve with lemon wedges on the side for squeezing.

Note: The dried chickpeas can be replaced with two 400-g/14-oz cans of cooked chickpeas, drained and rinsed. You'll need to reduce the cooking time to 20 minutes.

This delicious Mexican stew is flavoursome and out of the ordinary – a great way to put a substantial meal on the table in no time. Be sure to use a good-quality mole paste for best results. Any leftover chicken can also be boned, shredded and wrapped up in warmed flour tortillas for a quick lunch or snack.

chicken mole

2 tablespoons vegetable or olive oil
I onion, finely chopped
1.3 kg/3 lbs chicken pieces with bones
200 g/1 cup good-quality mole poblano paste
chicken stock (see page 35) or water, as required
sea salt

To serve
a few sprigs of fresh coriander/cilantro
sour cream
cooked rice mixed with finely chopped cooked spinach

Serves 4

Combine the oil and onion in the pressure cooker. Set on the stovetop over medium-high heat and cook for at least 10 minutes, stirring occasionally, until well coloured but taking care not to burn. The onion should be deep brown, caramelized and aromatic. Transfer to a plate, season with salt and set aside.

Add the chicken pieces to the cooker in a single layer and cook for 5–8 minutes, turning once, until browned on both sides. You may need to work in batches, depending on the size of your cooker.

Return the onions to the cooker and season lightly. Stir in the mole paste and dilute as required using the stock or water. The chicken pieces should be covered by at least 2 cm/¾ in so add more liquid if necessary.

Lock on the lid and bring to high pressure. Lower the heat slightly but maintain high pressure and cook under high pressure for 15 minutes then let cool naturally. When ready, release and remove the lid, taking care of any steam that is expelled as you open the pressure cooker.

Taste and adjust the seasoning. Divide the rice between warmed serving plates and top with the chicken. Garnish with sprigs of coriander/cilantro and serve with the sour cream on the side.

This is one of the most famous Italian summer dishes and is delightful made with turkey breast instead of more traditional veal. When cooked and cooled in the poaching liquid, it stays nice and moist. You'll need to start preparation two days before you plan to serve this dish. A simple tomato and red onion salad makes the ideal accompaniment.

turkey tonnato

1 kg/2 lb 4 oz skinless, boneless turkey breast
200 ml/¾ cup dry white wine
1 celery stalk, roughly chopped
1 carrot, roughly chopped
1 small onion, roughly chopped
1 bay leaf
2 whole cloves

For the mayonnaise sauce
250 g/1 cup good-quality canned tuna steak in oil, drained
6 anchovies in oil, rinsed
1 tablespoon salted capers, rinsed,
yolks from 3 hard-boiled/ cooked eggs
250 ml/1 cup olive oil
freshly squeezed juice of 1 lemon
2 teaspoons white wine vinegar
sea salt and freshly ground black pepper

To serve
1 lemon, thinly sliced
a handful of salted capers, rinsed

Serves 6

Two days before serving, put the turkey in a large bowl with the wine, celery, carrot, onion, bay leaf and cloves. Mix well, cover and let marinate in the refrigerator for 24 hours.

The day before serving, remove the turkey from the marinade and tie it up neatly with kitchen twine. Put the turkey in the pressure cooker. Pour in the marinade and vegetables, then top up with 200 ml/¾ cup water.

Lock on the lid and bring to high pressure. Lower the heat slightly but maintain high pressure and cook under high pressure for 30 minutes. Cool down naturally. When cool, release and remove the lid, taking care of any steam that is expelled as you open the pressure cooker.

Let the turkey cool in the cooking liquid. When cold, remove from the liquid. Wrap in kitchen foil and leave to chill until needed. Strain the liquid and chill for a couple of hours to allow any fat to set. When chilled, remove any fat from the surface of the liquid and and set aside.

To make the mayonnaise sauce, put the tuna, anchovies, capers, and egg yolks in a blender or food processor and blend until smooth. With the machine running, add the olive oil in a thin stream until it has all been absorbed and the mixture is thick and smooth. Scrape into a bowl and season to taste with the lemon juice and vinegar. Using the poaching liquid, carefully dilute the sauce until it is the right flowing consistency. Taste and adjust the seasoning with salt and pepper.

Slice the turkey thinly. Spread a few tablespoons of the sauce on a large, flat serving dish. Add a layer of turkey followed by a layer of sauce and continue until all is used up, finishing with sauce. Top with lemon slices and scatter over a handful of capers. Serve with a tomato and onion salad on the side, if liked.

A simple and tasty supper that can be ready in no time. This curry can also be made with boneless lamb, thinly sliced beef or even boneless skinless duck breast. Most supermarkets now stock good-quality curry paste and fish sauce so these ingredients are easy to find.

Thai green chicken curry

1 tablespoon vegetable oil

1 large shallot (or small onion), finely chopped

25-g/1-oz piece fresh ginger, grated

4–6 tablespoons Thai green curry paste, to taste

800 g/1 lb 12 oz boneless skinless chicken, preferably thigh meat, cut into bite-size pieces

800 ml/3¼ cups canned coconut milk

125 ml/1 cup chicken stock

1 tablespoon soy sauce

3 tablespoons Thai fish sauce

300 g/2 cups mangetout/snow peas

200 g/2 cups beansprouts

leaves from 1 small bunch of fresh coriander/cilantro, chopped

To serve
cooked white rice

5–6 spring onions/scallions, sliced on the diagonal

lime wedges

Serves 4

Put the oil and shallot in the pressure cooker. Set on the stovetop over medium heat and cook for 3–5 minutes until just golden. Stir in the ginger and curry paste and cook for 1 minute.

Add the chicken and cook for 1–2 minutes, stirring to coat well. Add the coconut milk and stock.

Lock on the lid and bring to high pressure. Lower the heat slightly but maintain high pressure and cook under high pressure for 10 minutes then let cool naturally. When cool, release and remove the lid, taking care of any steam that is expelled as you open the pressure cooker.

Stir in the soy sauce, fish sauce, mangetout/snow peas and beansprouts and cook for 2–3 minutes without the lid, until the vegetables are piping hot but still slightly crisp. Taste and adjust the seasoning, adding more soy or fish sauce as required.

Stir in half of the chopped coriander/cilantro and the spring onions/scallions. Spoon onto warmed serving plates. Sprinkle with the remaining spring onions/scallions and serve with rice and lime wedges for squeezing.

This deliciously spiced chicken is traditionally roasted in the oven, but you can achieve great results in a pressure cooker as it keeps the meat moist and only takes half the time.

whole Indian spiced chicken

1.5 kg/3 lb 5 oz chicken, skin removed

For the marinade
6 tablespoons plain yogurt
25-g/1-oz piece fresh ginger, grated
2 garlic cloves, crushed or finely chopped
2 teaspoons turmeric
2 teaspoons mild chilli powder
2 teaspoons hot paprika

For the onion spice paste
125 g/4 oz roughly chopped onions
2 garlic cloves, peeled and roughly chopped
25-g/1-oz piece fresh ginger, roughly chopped
2 teaspoons ground cumin
2 teaspoons ground coriander
½ teaspoon turmeric
2 teaspoons sweet paprika
¼ teaspoon cayenne pepper
2 generous tablespoons flaked/slivered almonds
3 tablespoons vegetable oil or ghee (clarified butter)
2 tablespoons freshly squeezed lemon juice
½ teaspoon garam masala
sea salt and freshly ground black pepper
lemon wedges, to serve

Serves 4–6

Skin the chicken starting at the breast and working down over the legs. Use a clean kitchen towel to help you grasp the skin.

Next, make the marinade by mixing all the ingredients together. Rub the paste all over the skinned chicken (inside and out) and set aside in a cool place to marinate for 2 hours.

Meanwhile, to make the onion spice paste put the onions, garlic, ginger, cumin, ground coriander, turmeric, paprika, cayenne pepper, almonds and 1¼ teaspoons salt into a food processor and whizz until smooth. Put the oil or ghee into the bottom of the pressure cooker and set on the stovetop. Add the onion spice paste and cook over medium heat for 8–9 minutes, until golden and aromatic. Add the lemon juice, garam masala and black pepper to taste and mix well. Scrape the paste out into a bowl and cool. There is no need to wash the pressure cooker.

Spread or rub the cooled onion spice paste all over the chicken, including the insides. Place the trivet in the pressure cooker and rest the chicken on top. Pour in 90 ml/⅓ cup water. Lock on the lid and bring to high pressure. Lower the heat slightly but maintain high pressure and cook under high pressure for 25 minutes. Let cool down naturally. When ready, release and remove the lid, taking care of any steam that is expelled as you open the pressure cooker.

Meanwhile, preheat the grill/broiler. Lift out the chicken and transfer to a grill pan then place under the grill/broiler to lightly brown the top. While the chicken is grilling, remove the trivet and pour out the cooking juices into a warm jug/pitcher.

Serve the chicken with the aromatic juices from the cooker, drizzled with the lemon juice and dusted with garam masala. Offer lemon wedges on the side for squeezing.

This classic American recipe works brilliantly in a pressure cooker. Ham is the traditional ingredient, but it is also common to use smoked sausage such as andouille from Louisiana.

jambalaya

1 tablespoon vegetable oil
1 kg/2 lbs 4 oz small chicken
  pieces (half thighs and
  half breasts)
1 large onion, chopped
1 orange bell pepper,
  coarsely chopped
1 green bell pepper,
  coarsely chopped
3 celery stalks, chopped
280 g/2 cups diced
  thick-sliced ham
2–3 garlic cloves, sliced
½ teaspoon smoked sweet
  paprika
a pinch of dried chilli/hot
  pepper flakes
200 g/1¼ cup basmati rice
400-g/14-oz can chopped
  tomatoes
1 teaspoon salt
1 bay leaf
200 g/7 oz frozen
  prawns/shrimp
sea salt and freshly ground
  black pepper

Serves 4–6

Pour the oil into the pressure cooker and set on the stovetop over medium heat. When hot, add the chicken pieces to the pressure cooker in a single layer and cook for 5–8 minutes, turning once, until browned on both sides. Depending on the size of your cooker, you may need to work in batches. Transfer to a plate, season with salt and set aside.

Add the onion, peppers and celery and cook over medium-high heat. Cook for at least 10 minutes, stirring occasionally, until well coloured but taking care not to burn. The vegetables should be deep brown, caramelized and aromatic.

Stir in the ham, garlic, paprika, dried chilli/hot pepper flakes and rice and cook for about 2 minutes, stirring to scrape up any browned bits. Add the tomatoes, 250 ml/1 cup water, salt and the bay leaf.

Arrange the chicken on top of the rice mixture and top with the prawns/shrimp. Lock on the lid and bring to high pressure. Lower the heat slightly but maintain high pressure and cook under high pressure for 15 minutes then let cool naturally. When cool, release and remove the lid, taking care of any steam that is expelled as you open the pressure cooker.

Stir to combine and adjust the seasoning if necessary. Spoon onto warmed serving plates and serve immediately.

This is an ideal weeknight meal when supplies run low since it can be made almost entirely from storecupboard and freezer ingredients. For a bit of additional greenery, you could throw in a large handful of defrosted frozen peas just before serving, or top with a few finely sliced spring onions/scallions for added crunch.

seafood curry

1 onion, finely chopped
1 tablespoon vegetable oil
2 garlic cloves, crushed
25-g/1-oz piece of fresh ginger, grated
1 fresh red chilli/chile, deseeded and finely chopped
1 teaspoon ground turmeric
2 teaspoons ground cumin
2 teaspoons ground coriander seeds
1 teaspoon hot paprika
400 ml/1⅔ cups canned coconut milk
800 g/1 lb 12 oz peeled prawns/shrimp, fresh or frozen
a handful of fresh coriander/cilantro leaves, finely chopped
sea salt and freshly ground black pepper

To serve
cooked basmati rice
a few sprigs of fresh coriander/cilantro

Serves 4

Put the onion and oil in the pressure cooker. Set over medium heat and cook for 3–5 minutes until just soft. Stir in the garlic, ginger, chilli/chile, turmeric, cumin, ground coriander seeds and paprika and cook for 1 minute, stirring continuously.

Add the coconut milk and prawns/shrimp. Lock on the lid and bring to high pressure. Lower the heat slightly but maintain high pressure and cook under high pressure for 4 minutes then let cool naturally. When cool, release and remove the lid, taking care of any steam that is expelled as you open the pressure cooker.

Remove the prawns/shrimp from the sauce and whisk the sauce well before serving to thicken. Taste and adjust the seasoning if necessary. Stir in the chopped coriander/cilantro. Divide the basmati rice between warmed serving plates, spoon over the curry and garnish with sprigs of coriander/cilantro to serve.

vegetarian dishes

This festive and aromatic curry can be served as a main dish or a side but it should be offered at room temperature to best appreciate the flavours. It is perfect for parties or large gatherings or great to have on hand for lunches or light meals.

chickpea curry with coconut and tamarind

1¼ tablespoons black mustard seeds

1¼ tablespoons cumin seeds

6 tablespoons vegetable oil

2 garlic cloves, crushed

4 tablespoons dessicated coconut/dried shredded coconut

2 tablespoons sesame seeds

2 tablespoons garam flour

½ teaspoon ground turmeric

½ teaspoon dried chilli/hot pepper flakes

1 fresh green chilli/chile, deseeded and finely chopped

200 ml/1 cup passata (Italian sieved tomatoes)

3 tablespoons tamarind concentrate

200 g/1 cup dates, pitted and finely chopped

370 g/2 cups dried chickpeas

1½ teaspoons sea salt

2 tablespoons sugar

To serve
plain yogurt
a large bunch of fresh coriander/cilantro, chopped

Serves 6–8

Combine the mustard and cumin seeds in a small frying pan and toast over low heat until the seeds become aromatic and begin to pop. Set aside to cool.

Put the oil, garlic, coconut, sesame seeds, garam flour, turmeric dried chilli/hot pepper flakes and fresh chilli/chile in the pressure cooker. Set on the stovetop over medium heat and cook for 2–3 minutes until aromatic.

Stir in the passata, tamarind, dates, 2 tablespoons of the toasted mustard and cumin seeds (reserving the rest to serve), chickpeas, half of the fresh coriander/cilantro and 1 litre/4 cups water. Mix to combine.

Lock on the lid and bring to high pressure. Lower the heat slightly but maintain high pressure and cook under high pressure for 50 minutes. Cool down using the quick cool method. When cool, release the lid, taking care of steam when removing.

Taste the chickpeas. If they are not completely tender, repeat the pressure cooking process for a further 10 minutes.

Stir in the salt and sugar. Taste and adjust the seasoning as necessary. Serve at room temperature topped with plain yogurt and sprinkled with chopped fresh coriander/cilantro and the reserved toasted cumin and mustard seeds.

This delicious mix of vegetables and rice looks and tastes complicated but it couldn't be easier to make. It is ideal for speedy weeknight suppers or late night snacks, either on its own or to accompany grilled meats or seafood.

mushroom, spinach and carrot biryani

2 tablespoons vegetable oil

I small onion, diced

250 g/2½ cups halved and sliced mushrooms

I large carrot, peeled and grated

300 g/1½ cups basmati rice

2–3 teaspoons hot curry powder

I fresh red chilli/chile, deseeded and finely diced

2 cardamom pods, crushed

a pinch of saffron

25-g/1-oz piece of fresh ginger, grated

500 ml/2 cups chicken or vegetable stock (see pages 32–35)

2 teaspoons sea salt

150 g/5 cups fresh spinach leaves

50 g/⅓ cup cashew nuts (optional)

a large handful of chopped fresh coriander/cilantro

a large handful of chopped fresh mint

Serves 4–6

Combine the oil, onion, mushrooms and carrot in the pressure cooker. Set on the stovetop over high heat and cook for 5–8 minutes, stirring occasionally, until well coloured but taking care not to burn. The vegetables should be deep brown, caramelized and aromatic.

Stir in the rice, curry powder, chilli/chile, cardamom, saffron and ginger and cook for 1 minute, stirring to coat the rice with the oil.

Add the stock and salt (if the stock is already seasoned, add less salt). Lock on the lid and bring to high pressure. Lower the heat slightly but maintain high pressure and cook under high pressure for 25 minutes. Cool down using the quick cool method. When cool, release and remove the lid, taking care of any steam that is expelled as you open the pressure cooker.

Taste and adjust the seasoning. Stir in the spinach, return to the heat and cook for 3–5 minutes without the lid, stirring occasionally, until the liquid is almost completely absorbed and the spinach is cooked. Remove from the heat and let stand for 5–10 minutes.

Taste and adjust the seasoning and stir in the cashew nuts (if using) and chopped herbs. Spoon into warmed serving dishes and serve immediately.

This bright, herb-flecked risotto can be served as an appetizer, main dish or side. It tastes best cooked with fresh herbs, but one teaspoon each of any similar dried herbs can also be used for convenience, though avoid dried basil as this often tastes slightly bitter.

tomato & herb risotto with artichokes

3 tablespoons olive oil
1 large onion, finely chopped
3 garlic cloves, finely chopped
leaves from a small bunch of fresh thyme
leaves from a small bunch of fresh oregano
leaves from a few sprigs of fresh rosemary
a small bunch of fresh flat-leaf parsley, chopped
600 g/3 cups risotto rice
1.2 litres/5 cups chicken or vegetable stock (see pages 32–35)
400 ml/1 ½ cups passata (Italian sieved tomatoes)
400-g/14-oz can artichoke hearts, drained and quartered
sea salt and freshly ground black pepper

Serves 4–6

Combine the oil and onion in the pressure cooker and set on the stovetop over high heat. Cook for 5–8 minutes, stirring occasionally, until well coloured but taking care not to burn. The onions should be deep brown, caramelized and aromatic.

Stir in the garlic, thyme, oregano, rosemary and most of the parsley. Add the rice and cook for about 1 minute, stirring to coat the grains with the oil.

Add the stock and passata and stir to mix. Lock on the lid and bring to high pressure. Lower the heat slightly but maintain high pressure and cook under high pressure for 8 minutes. Cool down using the quick cool method. When cool, release and remove the lid, taking care of any steam that is expelled as you open the pressure cooker.

Taste and adjust the seasoning. Return to the heat and cook without the lid for 3–5 minutes, stirring occasionally, until the liquid is almost completely absorbed. Taste and adjust the seasoning. Stir in the artichoke hearts and let stand for 5–10 minutes.

Spoon into warmed serving dishes. Sprinkle over the remaining parsley and serve immediately.

It is hard to believe that risotto can be made without laborious stirring but it can be done in no time at all with a pressure cooker. This simple recipe demonstrates the basics of perfect risotto cooked in the pressure cooker with minimum effort.

vegetable risotto

2 tablespoons olive oil
1 small onion, diced
100 g/1 cup mushrooms,
  halved and sliced
1 large carrot, diced
2 garlic cloves, crushed
300 g/1½ cups risotto rice
800 ml/3¼ cups chicken
  or vegetable stock
  (see pages 32–35)
a large handful of shelled
  peas, fresh or frozen
a large handful of chopped
  fresh flat-leaf parsley
sea salt and freshly ground
  black pepper
finely grated Parmesan,
  to serve

Serves 4

Combine the oil, onion, mushrooms and carrot in the pressure cooker. Set over high heat and cook for 5–8 minutes, stirring occasionally, until well coloured but taking care not to burn. The vegetables should be deep brown, caramelized and aromatic.

Stir in the garlic and rice and cook for 1 minute, stirring the rice well to coat the grains with the oil.

Add the stock. Lock on the lid and bring to high pressure. Lower the heat slightly but maintain high pressure and cook under high pressure for 4 minutes. Cool down using the quick cool method. When cool, release and remove the lid, taking care of any steam that is expelled as you open the pressure cooker.

Taste and adjust the seasoning. Stir in the peas, return to the heat and cook for 3–5 minutes without the lid, stirring occasionally, until the liquid is almost completely absorbed. Taste and adjust the seasoning and let stand for 5–10 minutes.

Stir in the parsley and spoon the risotto into warmed serving dishes. Top with grated Parmesan and serve immediately.

A good Mediterranean ratatouille can take up to four hours to cook, but using the pressure cooker, it will take a quarter of the time! This delicious ratatouille is worth making at least a day in advance, so that the flavours mellow and deepen. Serve warm or at room temperature with your favourite lamb dishes or with simply cooked fish.

ratatouille

500 g/1 lb 2 oz aubergines/eggplant
500 g/1 lb 2 oz courgettes/zucchini
500 g/5 cups thinly sliced onions
2 garlic cloves, crushed
100 ml/⅓ cup dry white wine
200 ml/¾ cup extra virgin olive oil
1 tablespoon fresh rosemary and thyme leaves, chopped
1 bay leaf
2 teaspoons coriander seeds, lightly crushed
1 teaspoon sugar
½ teaspoon sea salt
¼ teaspoon black pepper
200 g/1 cup canned chopped tomatoes
2 large red bell peppers
a few drops of red wine vinegar
sea salt and freshly ground black pepper
chopped fresh mixed herbs, to serve

Serves 4–6

Cut the stems from the aubergines/eggplant and cut into 2.5-cm/1-in cubes and put them in a deep bowl filled with very salty water. Weigh down with a plate to keep submerged for 1 hour.

Cut the courgettes/zucchini into 2.5 cm/1 in cubes and place in a deep colander. Cover with salt and let stand for 30 minutes to draw out the bitter juices.

Combine the onions and garlic in the pressure cooker then add the wine, 2 tablespoons water and 4 tablespoons of the olive oil, the rosemary and thyme, bay leaf, coriander seeds, sugar, salt and black pepper. Stir well and set over medium heat. Cook for 10–15 minutes, stirring often, until the onions are soft and golden.

Stir in the tomatoes, lock on the lid and bring to high pressure. Lower the heat slightly but maintain high pressure and cook under high pressure for 20 minutes. Cool down using the quick cool method. When cool, release and remove the lid, taking care of any steam that is expelled as you open the pressure cooker. Pour the sauce into a bowl and rinse and dry the cooker.

Meanwhile, grill/broil the peppers until charred then leave them to cool. Heat the remaining oil in the pressure cooker and brown the aubergines/eggplant in batches. When the peppers are cool, remove the skins, pull out the stems, scrape out the seeds, cut into bite-size pieces and add to the browned aubergines/eggplant with all their juices.

Stir in the tomato mixture, lock on the lid and bring to high pressure. Lower the heat slightly but maintain high pressure and cook under high pressure for a further 15 minutes. Cool down using the quick cool method. When cool, release and remove the lid, taking care of any steam that is expelled as you open the pressure cooker.

Taste and adjust the seasoning and stir in a few drops of vinegar. Serve warm or at room temperature, scattered with the fresh herbs.

This recipe makes a delicious lunch or dinner for vegetarians. It has all the flavour of the Greek Islands – especially with the hint of cinnamon, a popular spice in Greek cooking. If you don't feel comfortable stacking the aubergines/eggplant, cook them in two batches.

Greek-style stuffed aubergines

2 tablespoons olive oil
1 small onion, chopped
2 garlic cloves, chopped
1 teaspoon dried oregano
½ teaspoon dried thyme
½ teaspoon ground
  cinnamon
2 large tomatoes, deseeded
  and chopped or 100g/½
  cup cherry tomatoes,
  halved
65 g/⅓ cup bulgur wheat
2 large aubergines/eggplant
100 g/4 oz feta or goat
  cheese, cubed
sea salt and freshly ground
  black pepper
a handful of fresh flat-leaf
  parsley, chopped

Serves 4

Heat the olive oil in the pressure cooker on the stovetop and add the onion and garlic. Cook for 1–2 minutes until golden then stir in the oregano, thyme, cinnamon, tomatoes and bulgur wheat.

Trim and cut the aubergines/eggplant in half lengthwise. Scoop out the centres leaving a good rim around the edges. Chop the scooped out flesh and add to the bulgur wheat mixture. Season with salt and pepper. Tip into a bowl and wipe out the pressure cooker.

Pile this mixture back into the aubergines/eggplant. Set the trivet into the base of the pressure cooker and arrange the aubergines/eggplant on top (you will have to carefully stack them). Pour 200 ml/¾ cup water into the base of the pressure cooker.

Lock on the lid and bring to low pressure. Lower the heat slightly but maintain low pressure and cook for 4 minutes. Cool using the quick cool method. When cool, release and remove the lid, taking care of any steam that is expelled as you open the pressure cooker.

Remove from the pressure cooker with the aid of a fish slice. Dot with cheese and finish off under the grill/broiler, if desired. Serve immediately, scattered with chopped parsley and freshly ground black pepper.

The pressure cooker is ideal for preparing root vegetables and grains, both of which traditionally require long cooking. Here, they are cooked separately and united on the plate as a salad, linked with a slightly sweet dressing to offset the earthy quinoa and highlight the beetroot. This is ideal for entertaining as all the components can be prepared in advance and the dish assembled at the last minute.

beetroot & quinoa salad

**4 large beetroot/beets,
    scrubbed and halved**
180 g/1 cup quinoa
**120 g/1¾ cups mixed baby
    salad leaves (including pea
    tops if possible)**
freshly ground black pepper
**a large handful of chopped
    fresh herbs, such as chives
    or parsley**

For the dressing
**2 tablespoons balsamic
    vinegar**
**2 teaspoons sherry or
    wine vinegar**
2 teaspoons sea salt
2 tablespoons clear honey
**8 tablespoons vegetable
    or rapeseed oil**

Serves 4

Place the trivet inside the pressure cooker with 250 ml/1 cup water and arrange the beetroot/beets on top. Lock on the lid and bring to high pressure. Lower the heat slightly but maintain high pressure and cook under high pressure for 10 minutes. Cool down using the quick cool method. When cool, release and remove the lid, taking care of any steam that is expelled as you open the pressure cooker. Remove the beetroot/beets and set aside to cool.

Combine the quinoa with 800 ml/3¼ cups water in the pressure cooker. Lock on the lid and bring to high pressure. Lower the heat slightly but maintain high pressure and cook under high pressure for 1 minute then let cool naturally. When cool, release and remove the lid, taking care of any steam that is expelled as you open the pressure cooker. Transfer the quinoa to a bowl to cool.

To prepare the dressing, whisk together the vinegars and salt. Add the honey and whisk well. Gradually add the oil 1 tablespoonful at a time, whisking well between each addition.

When ready to serve, slice the beetroot/beets into wedges. Toss the quinoa with 4 tablespoons of the dressing. Mix the greens with 2 tablespoons of the dressing in a separate bowl.

Divide the leaves between 4 serving plates and place a large spoonful of quinoa on top of the greens. Top with the beetroot/beets and drizzle over any remaining dressing. Serve immediately sprinkled wih the fresh herbs and plenty of freshly ground black pepper.

sides

Soft polenta is a delicious alternative to mashed potatoes, but it usually takes around 45 minutes to cook. With the help of the pressure cooker, it only takes 15 minutes. This recipe makes a lovely soft polenta, although it will thicken and set as it cools. Different herbs such as parsley, thyme, basil or even mint can be added to vary the flavour. It is very versatile and makes a perfect accompaniment to meat dishes and sausages, tomato sauces, mushroom dishes and fish stews.

polenta

2 teaspoons finely grated lemon zest
4 teaspoons dried oregano
freshly grated nutmeg, to taste
300 ml/2 cups coarse polenta/cornmeal
2 fresh red or green chillies/chiles, deseeded and finely chopped (optional)
sea salt, to taste
about 7 tablespoons butter, plus extra to serve

Serves 6

Pour 800 ml/3¼ cups water into the pressure cooker. Add 1 teaspoon salt and slowly bring to the boil.

Add the lemon zest, oregano and nutmeg. Working quickly, pour the polenta/cornmeal into the pressure cooker in a steady shower whilst whisking briskly with a large balloon whisk to prevent any lumps from forming, then add the chillies/chiles (if using).

Lock on the lid and bring to high pressure. Lower the heat slightly but maintain high pressure and cook under high pressure for 15 minutes. Let cool naturally. When cool, release and remove the lid, taking care of any steam that is expelled as you open the pressure cooker.

Add the butter and whisk well, or beat with a wooden spoon until smooth. Taste and adjust the seasoning. Top with extra butter, if desired and serve immediately.

This recipe is a much faster alternative to boiled artichokes, which can sometimes take as long as 45 minutes to cook. In the pressure cooker, the artichoke bases gently sauté in the fragrant oil whilst the leaves steam in the vapour. Sometimes diced pancetta and parsley are added to the oil, but I prefer them as nature intended, so that the full flavour of the artichokes and olive oil can be appreciated.

braised globe artichokes

6 unwaxed globe artichokes with stems
2 unwaxed lemons, sliced
6 tablespoons olive oil
sea salt and freshly ground black pepper

Serves 6

To prepare the artichokes, snap off all the thick outer leaves. Cut the tough tips off the remaining leaves and trim the stems close to the base. Set the stems to one side to reserve for cooking – the stems are just as delicious as the base of the artichokes. Put 2 sliced lemons in a basin of cold water and add the artichokes. Using a potato peeler, peel the stems and drop them into the water.

Drain the artichokes and fit them snugly standing upright in the pressure cooker, pushing the peeled stalks in the spaces between them (if they are large you will have to cook them in two batches of three). Pour in the olive oil and season with salt and pepper. Set on the stovetop over medium heat and cook for about 15 minutes until the bottoms are nicely browned. Pour in 150 ml/⅔ cup water, lock on the lid and bring to high pressure. Lower the heat slightly but maintain high pressure and cook under high pressure for 4–8 minutes depending on the size of the artichokes. Cool down using the quick cool method. When ready, release and remove the lid, taking care of any steam that is expelled as you open the pressure cooker.

By this time the artichokes should be beautifully tender and the leaves should pull away with little or no resistance.

Serve warm with the cooking juices mixed with olive oil, salt and freshly ground black pepper for dipping.

These potatoes are cooked in a delicious Mediterranean-style sauce. They are the perfect accompaniment to roasted or grilled fish, but can also be served as a main dish, with steamed broccoli and a salad on the side.

new potatoes with tomato, bell pepper & olive sauce

1 onion, coarsely diced
1 red bell pepper, diced
1 yellow bell pepper, diced
2 tablespoons olive oil
3–4 garlic cloves, sliced
1 teaspoon dried oregano or thyme, plus extra to serve
630 g/2⅔ cups canned chopped tomatoes
100 g/½ cup pitted green olives, halved
¼ teaspoon dried chilli/hot pepper flakes
1 teaspoon sea salt
a pinch of sugar (optional)
650 g/1 lb 7 oz small new potatoes, scrubbed
sea salt and freshly ground black pepper

Serves 4–6

In a shallow saucepan, combine the onion, peppers and oil. Set on the stovetop over medium heat and cook for at least 10 minutes, stirring occasionally, until well coloured but taking care not to burn. The vegetables should be deep brown, caramelized and aromatic.

Stir in the garlic and oregano and cook for 1 minute more. Stir in the tomatoes and olives, dried chilli/hot pepper flakes and salt and simmer gently for 10–15 minutes. Taste and adjust the seasoning and add the sugar to reduce the acidity, if necessary.

To cook the potatoes, place 250 ml/1 cup water in the pressure cooker with the trivet in place. Add the potatoes, lock on the lid and bring to high pressure. Lower the heat slightly but maintain high pressure and cook under high pressure for 5–7 minutes then let cool naturally. When cool, release and remove the lid, taking care of any steam that is expelled as you open the pressure cooker.

Test the potatoes with a skewer. If they are not cooked through, repeat the pressure cooking process for a further 2–3 minutes.

Taste and adjust the seasoning. Spoon into a warmed serving dish and serve hot, sprinkled with extra dried oregano or thyme.

This is the recipe that converted me to using the pressure cooker because I discovered I was able to cook with dried beans in a fraction of the time. Butter bean purée is an ideal partner for any lamb dish but is equally good as part of a vegetarian meal or meze.

butter bean purée

275 g/1½ cups dried butter
  beans
1 bay leaf
1 onion, finely chopped
2 tablespoons olive oil
leaves from a few sprigs
  of fresh thyme, chopped
leaves from a few sprigs
  of fresh oregano, chopped
leaves from1 large sprig
  of fresh rosemary,
  chopped
leaves from 1 large sprig
  of fresh sage, finely
  chopped
4 garlic cloves, finely
  chopped
freshly squeezed juice of ½
  a lemon, or more to taste
sea salt and freshly ground
  black pepper

To serve
1–2 tablespoons sun-dried
  tomato paste, or 80 g/
  ¼ cup sun-dried
  tomatoes in oil, very
  finely chopped
1 tablespoon of extra virgin
  olive oil
a large handful of fresh
  flat-leaf parsley, chopped

Serves 4–6

Put the beans in the pressure cooker with 1.5 litres/6 cups water and the bay leaf.

Lock on the lid and bring to high pressure. Lower the heat slightly but maintain high pressure and cook under high pressure for 30 minutes. Cool down using the quick cool method. When cool, release and remove the lid, taking care of any steam that is expelled as you open the pressure cooker.

Test the beans. If they are not fully cooked, repeat the pressure cooking process for a further 10–15 minutes.

Meanwhile, in a deep frying pan, combine the onion and oil and set on the stovetop over medium heat. Cook for 5–10 minutes, stirring occasionally, until well coloured but taking care not to burn. The onion should be deep brown, caramelized and aromatic.

Stir in the herbs and cook for 3–5 minutes. Stir in the garlic and cook for 1 minute further, taking care not to burn. Season lightly with salt and set aside.

Drain the beans and reserve the cooking liquid. Work in batches using a food processor or hand-held blender to purée the beans. Add batches of beans to the bowl of the processor with enough of the reserved liquid to blend to a thick, smooth purée. Take care when doing so if the mixture is hot.

Transfer the beans to the pan with the onion. Add 2 teaspoons salt, stir well and taste. If the purée is too thin, continue simmering gently, stirring often, to thicken slightly. Stir in the lemon juice and adjust the seasoning as required.

Spoon the purée into a warmed serving bowl and top with the sun-dried tomatoes in the middle, stirring slightly to swirl. Drizzle over about 1 tablespoon olive oil and serve sprinkled with the parsley and freshly ground black pepper.

This classic dish can be served at any time of day with breakfast, lunch or dinner. Making this at home is much healthier than buying the canned alternative as cooking the beans in apple juice ensures they derive sweetness mainly from fruit, not from refined sugar. It is well worth making a big batch as it keeps well and can even be frozen in serving size portions for greater convenience.

baked beans

275 g/1½ cups dried haricot or cannellini beans
1 litre/4 cups apple juice
1 tablespoon dark brown sugar
1 teaspoon cider vinegar
3 tablespoons tomato ketchup
a pinch of ground allspice
1 teaspoon sea salt
1 teaspoon Worcestershire sauce

Serves 4–6

Put the beans and apple juice in the pressure cooker with 500 ml/2 cups water.

Lock on the lid and bring to high pressure. Lower the heat slightly but maintain high pressure and cook under high pressure for 30 minutes. Cool down using the quick cool method. When cool, release and remove the lid, taking care of any steam that is expelled as you open the pressure cooker.

Drain the beans and return them to the pot, reserving the cooking liquid.

Stir in the sugar, vinegar, tomato ketchup, allspice, salt and Worcestershire sauce. Add enough cooking liquid to barely cover the beans and simmer uncovered on the stovetop over low heat for 10–15 minutes, until slightly thickened. Taste and adjust the seasoning, adding more salt, sugar or vinegar to taste. The beans will thicken even more on standing so do not cook down too much; if it does, dilute with additional apple juice.

Serve as part of a hearty breakfast with fried eggs, bacon and wholemeal/wholewheat toast, or as desired.

This colourful and delicious salad is made with wild rice. It has a special chewy nuttiness and can be cooked to perfection in half the time in the pressure cooker. With nuts, carrots, mango, rocket/arugula and pomegranate seeds, this salad makes a special lunch dish or stunning buffet dish for a party.

wild rice, mint and pomegranate salad

170 g/⅔ cup wild rice
100 g/⅔ cup soft dried mango, peach or apricots, soaked in hot water for 5 minutes
50 g/½ cup shelled pine nuts, pistachios or pumpkin seeds
2 carrots, finely diced
3 spring onions/scallions, roughly chopped
a large handful of fresh mint leaves
1 small bunch of rocket/arugula or watercress

For the pomegranate dressing
4 tablespoons pomegranate molasses (or the finely grated zest and juice of 1 unwaxed lemon)
4 tablespoons extra virgin olive oil
2 large garlic cloves, crushed
75 g/⅔ cup fresh pomegranate seeds
sea salt and freshly ground black pepper

Serves 4

Put the rice in the pressure cooker and add 750 ml/3 cups cold water. Lock on the lid and bring to high pressure. Lower the heat slightly but maintain high pressure and cook under high pressure for 22 minutes. Cool down using the quick cool method. When cool, release and remove the lid, taking care of any steam that is expelled as you open the pressure cooker. Drain the rice and rinse under cold water. Season with salt and pepper.

While the rice is cooking, soak the dried mango in warm water for 10 minutes, then drain and roughly chop. Toast the nuts until lightly golden in a dry frying pan, stirring all the while to prevent them from burning. Transfer to a plate and let cool.

Tip the rice into a mixing bowl and add the chopped mango, nuts, carrots, spring onions/scallions, mint and rocket/arugula.

Put the dressing ingredients in a small bowl and whisk together until incorporated. Add salt and pepper to taste and pour over the salad. Toss to coat everything with the dressing.

Tip onto a large serving dish and arrange rocket/arugula leaves around the edges. Scatter with the fresh pomegranate seeds and serve immediately.

An entire cooked cauliflower makes a spectacular presentation dish. When I was a young girl living in France, it was usually served as an appetizer, with a bowl of thick mustardy vinaigrette for drizzling, but I prefer dipping the florets in a well-seasoned garlicky mayonnaise. Both recipes are provided so you can choose your favourite.

cauliflower with two sauces

1 cauliflower, not larger than the diameter of the pressure cooker

For the mayonnaise
4–6 tablespoons good quality mayonnaise
1–2 garlic cloves, crushed
1 teaspoon freshly squeezed lemon juice
2 tablespoons chopped fresh flat-leaf parsley

For the vinaigrette
3 teaspoons Dijon mustard
1 teaspoon fine sea salt
2 tablespoons wine or Sherry vinegar
10 tablespoons extra virgin olive oil
freshly ground black pepper

Serves 2–4

Remove the outer leaves from the cauliflower and trim the base. Fill the bottom of the pressure cooker with just enough water to reach the top of the trivet, making sure to use at least the minimum manufacturer's recommended amount. Set the cauliflower on top of the trivet.

Lock on the lid and bring to high pressure. Lower the heat slightly but maintain high pressure and cook under high pressure for 5 minutes. Cool down using the quick cool method. When cool, release and remove the lid, taking care of any steam that is expelled as you open the pressure cooker.

Test the cauliflower by piercing the underside of the base with a sharp knife. If it is not tender, repeat the pressure cooking process for a further 1–2 minutes. Let the cauliflower cool while you prepare the sauces.

For the mayonnaise, combine all the ingredients in a small bowl and mix well. Taste and adjust the seasoning.

For the vinaigrette, put the mustard, salt and vinegar in a small bowl and mix well with a whisk to dissolve the salt. Continue whisking and begin adding the oil, 1 tablespoon at a time, whisking well between each addition so the mixture thickens and stir in a few grinds of pepper. Taste and adjust the seasoning.

Serve the cauliflower just warm, or at room temperature, accompanied by the sauces for dipping.

desserts

These sticky marmalade cakes are a classic British dessert. This recipe quantity fills six individual metal pudding basins. Four fit comfortably in the pressure cooker, but six will fit if carefully stacked.

sticky marmalade cakes

150 g/2 cups fresh
    breadcrumbs
3 tablespoons plain/
    all-purpose flour
1 teaspoon baking powder
120 g/¾ cup dark brown
    sugar
6 tablespoons unsalted
    butter, melted, plus
    extra for greasing
7 tablespoons orange
    marmalade
3 eggs, beaten
finely grated zest and
    freshly squeezed juice
    of 1 unwaxed orange
custard sauce or pouring
    cream, to serve

6 individual metal pudding
    basins that will fit inside
    the pressure cooker

Serves 6

Generously grease 6 individual metal pudding basins with butter and set aside.

In a mixing bowl, combine the breadcrumbs, flour, baking powder and sugar and mix well.

Stir in the melted butter, 3 tablespoons of the marmalade, the eggs, orange zest and juice and stir to combine.

Divide the remaining marmalade between each of the prepared pudding basins and add the breadcrumb mixture.

Butter 6 pieces of foil – one to cover each of the puddings. Put a piece of baking parchment on top of the buttered side of each piece of foil and fold to form a pleat in the middle (to allow for expansion). Place the cover, baking parchment side down, on top of each of the puddings. Secure the foil under the rim of each pudding basin with kitchen twine.

Put the puddings in the pressure cooker, lock on the lid and bring to high pressure. Lower the heat slightly but maintain high pressure and cook under high pressure for 30 minutes then let cool naturally. When cool, release and remove the lid, taking care of any steam that is expelled as you open the pressure cooker.

Using kitchen tongs, carefully remove the puddings from the pressure cooker. Remove the foil and parchment lids and run a knife around the side of each pudding. Holding a plate against the top of each basin, invert onto individual serving plates and spoon over any marmalade remaining in the pudding basins. Serve hot or warm, with plenty of custard sauce or cream.

This is a much lighter and more delicate version of the traditional New York-style cheesecake made with cream cheese. Although this dessert feels summery, thanks to the berries, it can be made any time of year using frozen fruit with equal success.

mascarpone and ricotta cheesecake with blueberry compote

175 g/6 oz digestive biscuits/graham crackers, crushed (about 10)
5 tablespoons unsalted butter, melted, plus extra for greasing
250 g/1 cup ricotta
250 g/1 cup mascarpone
100 g/½ cup crème fraîche or thick plain yogurt
120 g/½ cup granulated sugar
4 eggs
freshly squeezed juice of a lemon

For the compote
250 g/2½ cups blueberries, fresh or frozen
150 g/⅔ cup caster/ superfine sugar
1 tablespoon cornflour/ cornstarch

a 20-cm/8-in springform cake pan that will fit inside your pressure cooker, greased

Serves 6–8

Take a very long piece of foil and fold to form a long thin strip. Use this to create a handle to allow you to raise and lower the filled cake pan from the pressure cooker. Set aside.

Mix the digestive biscuits/graham crackers and melted butter and press into the cake pan. Wrap the bottom of the pan in foil to prevent any moisture from leaking onto the crust and set aside.

Combine the ricotta, mascarpone, crème fraîche, sugar, eggs and lemon juice in a mixing bowl. With an electric mixer, or a whisk, beat until fluffy and doubled in volume.

Put 500 ml/2 cups water in the pressure cooker put the trivet on top. Set the prepared cake pan on top of the foil strip in the middle. Pour the cream cheese mixture into the pan and spread evenly. Bring up the strips to form a handle and use this to help you lower the pan into the pressure cooker, on top of the trivet.

Lock on the lid and bring to high pressure. Lower the heat slightly but maintain high pressure and cook under high pressure for 25 minutes then let cool naturally. When cool, release and remove the lid, taking care of any steam that is expelled as you open the pressure cooker.

In a saucepan, combine the blueberries, sugar and 125 ml/ ½ cup water and set on the stovetop. Bring to the boil over low heat and simmer gently for 1–2 minutes, then strain and return the juice to the pan. Set the blueberries aside in a bowl. Whisk the cornflour/cornstarch into the strained juice and bring to the boil. Reduce the heat and simmer for 1 minute then pour over the blueberries. Let cool until needed.

Using the foil handle, carefully lift out the cheesecake. Remove the foil from the bottom of the pan. Let cool slightly then release the sides of the pan and set on a wire rack to cool. Serve chilled, topped with the blueberry compote.

Everyone adores this silky baked egg custard with its integral caramel sauce. It can take a long time to cook in the oven but only takes 5 minutes in the pressure cooker! Although it is nice to make this in individual moulds, bringing a whole crème caramel to the table in all its glory is a very special treat.

crème caramel

175 g/¾ cup caster/
   granulated sugar
1 teaspoon pure vanilla
   extract
6 large eggs plus 1 egg yolk,
   beaten
800 ml/2¾ cups whole milk

*1-litre/4-cup heatproof
soufflé dish, or similar, that
will fit inside your pressure
cooker*

Serves 8

To make the caramel, begin by filling a bowl with cold water. This will be used to cool the caramel and stop it from over-cooking. Sprinkle 125 g/½ cup sugar evenly over the base of a medium-size heavy-based saucepan or frying pan. Cook on the stovetop over very gentle heat until the sugar melts completely without boiling.

Turn the heat up slightly and boil gently until the sugar turns to a rich, golden caramel. As soon as it reaches this point, remove from the heat and dip the base of the pan in the bowl of cold water to stop the caramel over-browning. The caramel will set on the bottom so return the pan to the heat until it liquefies and then pour into a warmed heatproof soufflé dish and set aside.

Beat the eggs and extra yolk with the vanilla extract in a medium bowl or a large jug/pitcher until thoroughly mixed.

Gently heat the milk in a saucepan set on the stovetop with the remaining sugar, stirring occasionally until the sugar dissolves. Add the warm milk to the eggs and stir well. Pour this onto the caramel. Cover with foil. Take two very long pieces of foil and fold to form two long strips. Use these as handles to allow you to raise and lower the dish from the pressure cooker. Set the trivet in the base of the pressure cooker and carefully put the soufflé dish on top.

Pour 300 ml/1¼ cups water into the base of the pressure cooker. Lock on the lid and bring to high pressure. Lower the heat slightly but maintain high pressure and cook under high pressure for 5 minutes then let cool naturally. When cool, release and remove the lid, taking care of steam when removing. Remove the foil. Cool and chill for at least 2–3 hours or overnight to set.

When ready to serve, loosen around the sides with a thin-bladed knife. Place a serving dish on top and flip over quickly. The crème caramel will slip out, surrounded by its delicious caramel sauce. Serve immediately.

Pressure cookers are the best utensil for cooking rice quickly and this sweet version is no exception. This might just be one of the speediest dessert recipes ever. Chocolate sauce makes an indulgent alternative to the strawberry preserve.

rice pudding

750 ml/3 cups whole milk
3 tablespoons dark brown
sugar
2 tablespoons clear honey
½ teaspoon mixed spice/
apple pie spice
200 g/1 cup pudding rice
2 tablespoons unsalted
butter, melted

To serve
ground cinnamon
double/heavy cream
strawberry preserve

Serves 4–6

Combine the milk, sugar, honey, mixed spice/apple pie spice, rice and butter in the pressure cooker.

Lock on the lid and bring to high pressure. Cook under high pressure for 5 minutes then let cool naturally. When cool, release and remove the lid, taking care of any steam that is expelled as you open the pressure cooker.

Stir the rice and transfer to serving bowls. Dust very lightly with cinnamon and serve immediately, topped with cream and strawberry preserve.

There is not much time saved by cooking this in a pressure cooker. The real advantage is in the lovely velvety smooth texture which really brings out the apple flavour. The stovetop preparation is also especially useful if preparing a large family meal such as a roast and oven space is being used for other dishes.

apple-cinnamon bread and butter pudding

For the apples
3½ tablespoons unsalted butter, plus extra for greasing
350 g/12 oz apples, peeled and diced
4 tablespoons caster/superfine sugar

For the pudding
200 ml/¾ cup whole milk
200 ml/¾ cup double/heavy cream
3 large eggs
2 tablespoons sugar
¼ teaspoon ground cinnamon
4 slices wholemeal/wheat bread, halved
cream or custard sauce, to serve

a heatproof soufflé dish, or similar, that will fit inside your pressure cooker, generously greased

Serves 4–6

Take a very long piece of foil and fold to form a long thin strip. Use this to create a handle to allow you to raise and lower the filled dish from the pressure cooker. Set aside.

For the apples, melt the butter in a frying pan. Add the apples and sugar and stir to blend. Cook for 8–10 minutes, stirring rarely, until just caramelized. Remove from the heat and set aside.

Meanwhile, in a mixing bowl, combine the milk, cream, eggs, sugar and cinnamon and whisk to blend thoroughly. Set aside.

Put about 500 ml/2 cups water in the pressure cooker and place the trivet on top.

Set the prepared heatproof dish on top of the long foil strip in a central position. Transfer one third of the apple mixture to the bottom of the dish. Top with half of the bread slices and arrange half of the remaining apple on top. Cover with the remaining bread, then finish with the remaining apple. Pour the milk mixture over the top.

Bring up the strips of foil to form a handle and use this to help you lower the dish into the pressure cooker, on top of the trivet.

Lock on the lid and bring to high pressure. Lower the heat slightly but maintain high pressure and cook under high pressure for 30 minutes then let cool naturally. When cool, release the lid, taking care of steam when removing.

Using the foil handle, carefully lift out the pudding. Let cool slightly before spooning into warmed serving bowls and serve with cream or custard sauce.

This simple recipe is ideal when you need to whip up an elegant dinner party dessert in minutes. The pears are delicious on their own with just the poaching liquid but can also be served with cream or vanilla ice cream and slices of Madeira cake, or a few biscotti.

pears in spiced wine

750 ml/3 cups sweet white dessert wine
½ cinnamon stick
¼ teaspoon mixed spice/apple pie spice
4 medium pears of equal size, not too ripe
2 tablespoons granulated sugar

To serve
peel of I unwaxed orange
cinnamon sticks

Serves 4

Combine the wine and spices in the pressure cooker, set over medium high heat and bring to the boil. Let stand for at least 15 minutes to allow the spices to permeate the wine.

Peel and core the pears and cut in half lengthwise.

Put the pears in the pressure cooker with the wine. Lock on the lid and bring to high pressure. Cook under high pressure for $2\frac{1}{2}$ minutes then let cool naturally. Release the lid, taking care of steam when removing.

Carefully remove the pears with a slotted spoon. Serve warm or at room temperature, with some of the poaching liquid garnished with strips of orange peel and cinnamon sticks.

Pressure cookers are ideal for preparing custard since the heat is very even, much like a bain marie. This creamy tart is best served warm – about half an hour after removing from the pressure cooker. For the crumb base, any kind of dry biscuit or cookie can be used – ginger- or almond-flavoured ones both work very well.

rich chocolate tart

For the crumb base
175 g/1¾ cups chocolate
   digestive biscuits/graham
   crackers, crushed
80 g/5 tablespoons unsalted
   butter, melted plus extra
   for greasing

For the filling
125 g/¾ cup
   dark/bittersweet
   chocolate, melted
150 ml/⅔ cup whole milk
150 ml/⅔ cup double/
   heavy cream
3 large eggs
100 g/½ cup caster/
   superfine sugar
4 tablespoons plain/
   all-purpose flour
grated chocolate,
   to decorate
whipped cream, to serve

*a 20-cm/8-in. springform
cake pan that will fit inside
the pressure cooker*

Serves 6–8

Take a very long piece of foil and fold to form a long thin strip. Use this to create a handle to allow you to raise and lower the cake pan from the pressure cooker. Set aside.

Prepare the crumb base. In a bowl, mix together the crushed biscuits/crackers and melted butter. Press into the cake pan in an even layer. Wrap the bottom of the pan in foil to prevent any moisture from leaking onto the crust. Ensure the foil wrapping does not prevent the pan from fitting into the cooker. Test before filling and adjust the wrapping if necessary. Set aside.

For the filling, combine the chocolate, milk, cream, eggs, sugar and flour in a mixing bowl. Using a whisk, beat until well blended.

Put 500 ml/2 cups water in the pressure cooker and put the trivet on top.

Set the cake pan on top of the foil strip in the middle. Pour the chocolate mixture into the pan. Bring up the strips to form a handle and use this to help you lower the pan into the pressure cooker, on top of the trivet.

Lock on the lid and bring to high pressure. Lower the heat slightly but maintain high pressure and cook under high pressure for 30 minutes then let cool naturally. When ready, release the lid, taking care of steam when removing.

Using the foil handle, carefully lift out the tart. Gently dab away any water on the surface with paper towels. Remove the foil from the bottom of the pan. Let the tart cool slightly, run a knife around the sides, then release the sides of the pan and set on a wire rack.

Serve garnished with grated chocolate with whipped cream.

This is an incredibly easy cake to prepare, despite its enticing appearance. Thanks to the pressure cooker, the result is an incredibly moist cake with a deliciously sticky topping.

banana upside-down cake

For the topping
75 g/5 tablespoons butter
100 g/½ cup soft dark
    brown sugar
2 bananas, sliced into
    thick rounds

For the cake batter
125 g/1 stick unsalted
    butter, softened, plus
    extra for greasing
125 g/½ cup caster/
    granulated sugar
2 eggs
250 g/2 cups plain/
    all-purpose flour
3 teaspoons baking powder
1–2 tablespoons milk

*a loose-bottomed cake pan
    that will fit inside your
    pressure cooker*

Serves 6–8

Take a very long piece of foil and fold to form a long thin strip. Use this to create a handle to allow you to raise and lower the cake pan from the pressure cooker. Set aside.

To make the topping, melt the butter and brown sugar in a small saucepan and set over low heat. Melt, stirring until fully blended. Bring to the boil and let bubble gently for 1 minute. Remove from the heat and set aside.

For the cake batter, beat together the butter and sugar. Add the eggs, one at a time.

Mix the flour and baking powder together in a separate bowl. Stir in the flour in two batches. Add 1 tablespoon milk. The batter should have a light dropping consistency. Add more milk if necessary.

Put 500 ml/2 cups water in the pressure cooker and put the trivet on top.

Set the cake pan on top of the foil strip in the middle. Transfer the brown sugar mixture to the pan and spread evenly. Arrange the banana slices on top. Put dollops of batter on top, then smooth over evenly.

Bring up the foil strips to form a handle and use this to help you lower the pan into the pressure cooker, on top of the trivet.

Lock on the lid and bring to high pressure. Lower the heat slightly but maintain high pressure and cook under high pressure for 30 minutes then let cool naturally. When cool, release and remove the lid, taking care of steam when removing.

Let cool for a further 5 minutes, then turn the cake out onto a serving plate. Serve at room temperature.

index

credits

All photographs by William Reavell
except pressure cooker images on pages 1 and 5 courtesy
of Kuhn Rikon, www.kuhnrikon.co.uk
Telephone +44 (0)1902 458410 for UK stockists or mail
order supplier.
For details of stockists in the US visit www.kuhnrikon.com

All jacket photography by William Reavell except back jacket
top left courtesy of Kuhn Rikon, www.kuhnrikon.co.uk